"Like 'a voice of one crying in the wi[...] goes out to churches seeking a parti[...] seeking discernment of journeying a[...] *The Church and Foster Care* is invitation, counsel, and primer. The book affirms many ways of responding *right where we live* to God's mandate to care for the youngest and most desperate. In clear, simple, and stimulating writing, he stirs the imagination and encourages honest response to God's call."

—REVEREND DR. CARL B. (JAKE) MARSHALL, Central Florida Presbytery, PCUSA

"Dr. DeGarmo's book, *The Church and Foster Care,* is amazing. As a foster parent, I find it to be inspirational and resourceful. As a churchgoer, I find it to be quite insightful. There are definitely elements I will take with me to church to better equip them to serve existing foster families and inspire other members to become foster families (or at least serve them as they can). The book is full of personal stories, Scripture, and resources. It will serve as a great tool for existing foster families needing motivation or inspiration and an excellent resource to tie foster care and the church together. It is a great read for anyone, regardless of their current level of involvement in foster care. I would highly recommend this book to everyone."

—ANTHONY CAMPAGNA, foster parent

"When John writes 'everyone can do something,' he has no shortage of examples reflecting the evidence of this statement. While peppered throughout with poignant stories and biblical mandates, *The Church and Foster Care* could be a welcomed resource even to those who do not adhere to a Christian worldview. That said, I believe this project should be close at hand to every child welfare agency and worker across the nation."

—MR. KIM COMBES, MEd, author, counselor, national presenter, and foster/adoptive parent

"Dr. DeGarmo's book is a wake-up call to our country concerning the desperate need for foster care that is unfortunately all around us. He and his wife probably know as much or more about foster children and foster parenting than anyone on the planet. I know them personally and if anybody ever 'walked the walk,' they certainly have. It's true that we all can't be foster parents, but with God's help, we can find ways to make a positive difference in the lives of thousands of precious children."

—JAMES COBB, retired writer/publisher

"Look, let's be honest. There are not a lot of books and resources out there helping foster parents navigate the highs and lows of fostering. John and Kelly have put in their 10,000 hours of love, joy, suffering, and faith to give children hope. Hope is like gold in the lives of children who come from difficult places. Every time I talk with a foster parent, John's name *always* comes up. You want to listen to someone who experiences foster parenting and has survived it!"

—GLENN GARVIN, speaker and writer

"Dr. DeGarmo brings home to us all what Jesus meant when He said, 'Let the little children come unto me!' With amazing clarity and insight, he reveals not only the depth of the need but also the call to the church to embrace foster children. There are more than 500,000 children in foster care nationwide. Dr. DeGarmo shows us how to be the arms and legs of Christ helping these children and planting the seed of faith in them."

—THE REV. KATHI PARCHEM, MDiv, Presbyterian minister and former moderator, Savannah Presbytery, PCUSA

"As a former student pastor and now as a lead pastor, I have sensed in my ministry over the years a growing trend among our youth seeking to be loved and encouraged. Sadly, this desire is fueled by a deficient home life. In his book, Dr. John DeGarmo brings to light the growing epidemic and the gut-wrenching challenges facing many children in foster care. At no fault of their own, many of these children have never experienced a loving and safe place to call home. For this reason, people of faith must step forward to engage with this problem. We must actively and intentionally meet the varied and growing needs of the children and the families in foster care. We must let the love of Christ, who reached out to all, shine through our churches and our individual lives to light a path to our Heavenly Father. After all, 'Pure and genuine religion in the sight of God the Father means caring for orphans . . . in their distress' (James 1:27 NLT). This book will bring you to tears, make you think, force you to your knees in prayer, and hopefully inspire you to assist in changing the lives of children in foster care."

—DAVID ARTESSA, pastor, Monticello Baptist Church, Monticello, GA

The Church & Foster Care

Dr. John DeGarmo

Other NewHope® Books by John DeGarmo

Faith and Foster Care: How We Impact God's Kingdom

THE
Church &
foster Care

GOD'S CALL TO A
GROWING EPIDEMIC

DR. JOHN DEGARMO

NEW HOPE
PUBLISHERS

New Hope® Publishers
5184 Caldwell Mill Rd.
Ste. 204-221
Hoover, AL 35244
NewHopePublishers.com
New Hope Publishers is an imprint of Iron Stream Media

Library of Congress Cataloging-in-Publication Data

Names: DeGarmo, John, 1969- author.
Title: The Church and foster care : God's call to a growing epidemic / John
    DeGarmo.
Description: First [edition]. | Birmingham : New Hope Publishers, 2018. |
    Includes bibliographical references and index.
Identifiers: LCCN 2018046319 (print) | LCCN 2018057532 (ebook) | ISBN
    9781563091155 (Ebook) | ISBN 9781563094712 (permabind : alk. paper)
Subjects: LCSH: Adoption—Religious aspects—Christianity. | Adoption—United
    States.
Classification: LCC HV875.26 (ebook) | LCC HV875.26 .D437 2018 (print) | DDC
    362.73/30973—dc23
LC record available at https://lccn.loc.gov/2018046319

ISBN-13: 978-1-56309-471-2
Ebook ISBN: 978-1-56309-115-5

1 2 3 4 5—23 22 21 20 19

For Daniela, who has shown me that with love and commitment, children in foster care can beat the system. You inspire me with your amazing story of success.

For I was hungry and you gave me something to eat,
I was thirsty and you gave me something to drink,
I was a stranger and you invited me in, I needed clothes and
you clothed me, I was sick and you looked after me,
I was in prison and you came to visit me.

—*Matthew 25:35–36*

CONTENTS

I would like to thank God for His love and wisdom during my journey as a foster parent and for His guidance with this book. I would also like to thank my children and my wife, who were patient as I wrote yet another book! Finally, thank you to all who contributed to this book with your personal stories. Each of you is not only an inspiration to many but also a light in the foster care world.

FOREWORD

Within both the Old and New Testaments, God's Word reflects His heart for us to defend, care for, and love the most vulnerable of the world. The Law says in Deuteronomy 10:18, "He defends the cause of fatherless." The prophets echo the same truth, "For in you the fatherless find compassion" (Hosea 14:3), while Psalm 68:5–6 says, "A father to the fatherless, a defender of the widows, is God in his holy dwelling."

Throughout Scripture, we see the gospel and truth of God's "father heart" as it beats equally for us as well as the marginalized orphan. Whether by fostering, adopting, mentoring, or volunteering, we display God's heart for others while experiencing God heart more deeply ourselves.

Those who have accepted His gift of love know He pursued us when we were broken, hurt, and abandoned—He adopted us as His children and He invites us to call Him Abba, Father. We are His sons and daughters, living in all authority and power as His heirs. What a powerful demonstration and picture of love God has given to us . . . God expects us to do the same by living out James 1:27, "Religion that God our Father accepts as pure and faultless is this: to look after orphans and widows in their distress."

Dr. John DeGarmo has been in constant pursuit of knowledge and best practices of the most cutting-edge foster care initiatives in America. His efforts, alongside his personal faith-filled journey as a foster parent, have helped him form a comprehensive understanding of how the church is engaging across America. His expertise allows his message to the church to be clear, applicable, and practical. His wide-ranging ideas place focus beyond the desperate need of families willing to foster and/or adopt. He looks at volunteer opportunities, foster care support initiatives, "aging out" efforts, and many other options available to anyone—not just the foster parent. It is perfectly clear God is not asking the church to reinvent itself to fit into needs of our failing foster care system. Rather, miracles happen when we invest our talents and gifts, of which God has already equipped the church with, to further the kingdom for the least of these.

When you consider the plethora of talents collective among us all, as well as the diverse talents of churches across America, it is easy to see how the body can provide solutions in perfect harmony with one another. While one church may have the talents of discipleship, allowing them to mentor foster youth and provide support and encouragement to foster parents, another church may have the talent of service (volunteering). In addition, some churches are financially gifted, and tangible items such as school supplies and Christmas gifts are easily donated in support of the children and families. Many of our churches are gifted with amazing children's church ministries that include Parents' Night Out, Vacation Bible School, camps, or festivals for foster children.

It is when we invest our given talents to further the kingdom that we see the gospel at work on earth as it is in heaven.

God never intended for the government alone to care for His children; it is the church's responsibility, and although not everyone is called to foster or adopt, we *are* all called to do *something*. Dr. DeGarmo sheds light on ways in which we can all engage in helping fulfill God's love for these children.

We are called to care for the orphan; *we* are called to care for the orphan; we are *called* to care for the orphan; we are *all called*.

I pray this book reaches into the hearts of its readers and activates them to invest even 10 percent of their talents into our failing foster care system. In doing that, we will see, "Thy kingdom come, Thy will be done in earth, as it is in heaven" (Matthew 6:10 KJV).

TERRI JAGGERS
Orphan Care Solutions of Texas, president
Texas Foster Parent Association, president

THE CHURCH & FOSTER CARE

DR. JOHN DEGARMO

TODAY'S FOSTER CARE

*T*hree children showed up at our door at 8:30 that winter evening. Like proverbial deer in headlights, they stared at us before we ushered them into our home. The look of fear was evident in each of their eyes. They were scared—of us perhaps? Of being removed from their home by the police? Of what they witnessed before they came to our home? I was unsure. All I knew was these three children were scared and needed a home immediately. More importantly, they needed someone to care for them.

According to the social worker, the thirteen-year-old boy, eleven-year-old girl, and ten-year-old boy had been living in a house of horrors. They suffered daily physical, verbal, and sexual abuse by the adults in their lives. Beatings and rape were common for all three. The home the children were staying at had no running water, no toilets, no electricity, no food, and no heat or air. A large blue tarp covered a large hole in one of the bedrooms, a meager attempt to keep the rain and weather out. Three deputy sheriffs had to go into the home and remove the children from a dangerous environment.

"In all my years as a social worker, I have never seen anything like this," Sharon, the children's caseworker, told my wife and me. "This was the most disturbing removal I have ever been part of." Sitting across the dining room table, the three of us were signing paperwork for our newest children from foster care. The three children were downstairs, playing with some of the other children in our home, while we quickly took care of the required documentation.

"I am not exaggerating when I tell you that it was the worst thing I have ever seen," she continued, her eyes reflecting shock of her own. "We could literally not see the floor in the house."

"What do you mean?" my wife Kelly asked, as she sat down her hot cup of tea. The two of us had been foster parents for eleven years at that point, with more than forty-five children coming through our home and into our lives. We had witnessed some horror stories of our own. "Why is that?" she again asked.

Sharon did not answer right away. Instead, she looked off into the distance, as though she were collecting her thoughts, and herself. After a moment, she looked at us, and her face easily expressed the horror she both saw and felt.

"It was . . . awful," she shuddered. "I can honestly tell you that you couldn't see any of the floor in the entire house, as there was so much feces covering the floor."

Stunned by this shocking revelation, I whispered aloud, "Feces? Human feces?"

Sharon's voice shook as she responded. "I think there was a lot of that, mixed in with dog feces. One of the deputies who went in had to walk back out of the house and take some time. He had become so horrified by the living conditions of these children he was becoming sick to his stomach."

Placing her hand to her mouth, Kelly was extremely, and understandably, distressed by the news. "Were the children," she paused, and took a deep breath before continuing. "Were they in the house with this mess?"

"Some were," responded the caseworker. "The older boy was sitting in a car, with one of his mother's teenage boyfriends. The two were acting as a lookout for the police. When the police arrived, the thirteen-year-old tried to run back into the house and warn his mother. The eleven-year-old girl was lying in a bed, which was covered in feces, while the ten-year-old was at another friend's house. The mother was also lying in a feces-covered bed with another boyfriend." After asking about the father, Sharon informed us he was nowhere to be found. The mother's current husband had pulled a knife on her the week before and had since disappeared. As a source of income, the mother had been running a meth lab in the house with her two teenage boyfriends, both only a few years older than the thirteen-year-old son.

Fifteen minutes after our three newest ones had arrived, we finished signing all the paperwork and said our goodbyes to Sharon. The children were incredibly hungry and incredibly filthy, and it appeared they hadn't had food or a shower in some time. Sandwiches were made, and like so many children from foster care who first enter our home, they devoured the food as soon as it was placed in front of them. Afterwards, as the three began showering, Kelly was on the phone with one of our fellow church members, answering various questions. Our church family had been quite supportive of our fostering over the years, in a number of ways. We could not have been the foster parents we are without the support, the love, and the prayers from our church.

As Kelly was on the phone, I sent our other children off to bed with hugs and kisses, and then I went in search of extra pajamas for the three newest family members. And they were just that—our newest family members. There are no labels in our home—no adoptive child, no biological child, no foster child—they are simply our children, and we love each of them unconditionally, just as God loves us. Finding some spare pajamas, I began to wash the children's clothes and jackets—the only possessions they had to call their own. When they first arrived, I noticed the clothing was in rough shape, as is often the case when children from foster care are first placed into our home. What surprised me about this lot of clothing was that much of it was stapled together, and of course the unmistakable odor of feces clinging to them.

These three children had arrived to our home from a house of horrors. These children had experienced things I did not wish to imagine. Yet what disturbed me the most was the fact that these children did not live in a third world country. What disturbed me was that these children not only lived in the United States of America, these three lived only five miles from my own home. These three had suffered unspeakable atrocities in my own town, just moments away from where my own children lived comfortable and secure lives.

Sadly, this is the reality of hundreds of thousands of children, not only around the world, but in our very hometowns. As I write this, and even as you read this, there are children in America who are having unthinkable crimes committed against them, not only by strangers, but by those who profess to love them the most—their family members.

When I was younger, I had several opportunities to travel outside the United States for mission trips. Each mission trip brought significant growth and life changing experiences in a number of ways. And while each trip had a purpose—an opportunity to help those in need—I found myself much more impacted by our work there.

However, it has been my experience as a foster parent the past fourteen years that has changed me the most. During that time, I have had more than forty-five children come to be a part of my family. Some have stayed only a day or two. Some have stayed up to two years. The youngest to be placed into my home was only twenty-seven hours old while the oldest was eighteen. Each child that has come to live with my family has made me a better father, a better husband, a better person. Has it always been easy? Definitely not. There have been those sleepless nights when I tried to comfort a crying and confused child. There have been those days when I struggled to help a child in need deal with the grief and heartbreak they felt when a birth parent did not show up for a visitation. There have been those times when my wife and I were simply exhausted from the day-to-day challenges that come with being a parent to up to ten children in the home. Yet being a foster parent has been the most rewarding thing I have ever done.

But it isn't for everyone.

Let's be clear; not everyone feels the calling to be a foster parent. And not everyone has the talents, the skills, and the desire to be a foster parent, to bring children into their home and care for those in need. God has blessed us all with different skills and talents. Some are able to care for children in their homes each day. Others are better able to financially support foster parents and care givers. Still others are able to provide help and resources. Scripture is clear on this.

> WE HAVE DIFFERENT GIFTS, ACCORDING TO THE GRACE GIVEN
> TO EACH OF US. IF YOUR GIFT IS PROPHESYING, THEN PROPHESY
> IN ACCORDANCE WITH YOUR FAITH; IF IT IS SERVING, THEN SERVE;
> IF IT IS TEACHING, THEN TEACH; IF IT IS TO ENCOURAGE, THEN
> GIVE ENCOURAGEMENT; IF IT IS GIVING, THEN GIVE GENEROUSLY;
> IF IT IS TO LEAD, DO IT DILIGENTLY; IF IT IS TO SHOW MERCY, DO
> IT CHEERFULLY. —ROMANS 12:6–8

DEANN'S STORY

—— o ——

Every mom has a story. My journey to where I am as a foster mom has been full of unexpected twists, sometimes messy and a bit confusing at times and yet unbelievably blessed all along. I've heard the best thing you do for the kingdom of God might not be what you do but who you raise. I am so thankful God chose to surround me with all of you along the way. Church, your love and patience for my kids and me has been such a treasure. This is what it means to be the family of God.

It is when you tell me your little ones still miss and remember my little ones even though mine moved away months ago. You keep me from feeling as though they have been forgotten. It is when you bring a kid a new coat, and she says she won't wear it because she thinks it's ugly. While I was still trying to decide how to tactfully rescue this conversation, you answered with enough grace and poise and patience to overshadow the fact that this kid hasn't ever been taught those traits.

It's cleaning out closets and toy boxes and giving a teenager her first curling iron for Christmas or a little girl new Easter sandals just because you thought she would like them. It's praying with wisdom when a kid with tears running down her cheeks asks you to pray for her family. You prayed eagerly, even though her family doesn't function like yours and what she is praying for her family may never be possible for her to have again. You gave her hope but didn't patronize her worries.

It is when you welcome a couple of kids who are only going to be here for one weekend and yet you invite them to your son's birthday party. You weren't ever going to meet these kids again, but you still made sure they were included for the short time they were here, and it was a highlight of their weekend.

It's a little girl learning to write, and her first complete story was, "Once upon a time, it was the best day ever at church." And it's me knowing that this is the only church she's been a part of. It's the day we were almost late to church, and I came in so frazzled with a crying kid in each hand. You met me at the door and recognized the same exhaustion and self-doubt every new mom faces. You took the kids and gave me permission to fall apart or put myself back together. You said you would watch over them for however long it took. You had no idea we had just spent thirty minutes sitting on the side of the road with a kid screaming, "You're not my mommy, and she doesn't make me wear a seatbelt so I don't have to." You didn't know the only reason we made it here at all that night was because it was so much closer than turning around and going home. You just knew I needed an understanding hug and permission not to have everything all together. It's a kid about to move several hours away, and she's trying to figure out if her new family will still drive her to this church sometimes because she says she will miss all of you too much.

It's you finding out a kid has never eaten a grapefruit, so you pull out your pocketknife to cut one open and share with her. It's a kid wondering what your whiskers feel like and immediately you answered her just like you would have if your own granddaughter had asked. You didn't hesitate; you just let her feel your bearded chin. You treated her curious question with as much respect as you would have given any kid you've ever known. It's having a kid ask to sit by you at church every week because you tug on her ponytail and tell her jokes before church just to see her smile.

It's having a special going away service for kids you might never see again. You told them how special they were and blessed them as they went out. I wrote that blessing in the front of their Bibles so they could always look back at it. I recently heard from them, and they are adopted into a stable, happy home, and their family says they still talk a lot about their time here. It's you helping plant the seeds of faith in their little hearts even if the fruit blossoms elsewhere.

For me, being part of this church family is seeing you do all these little things you didn't even realize you were doing to show such an incredible love to the kids God has given us the opportunity to minister to together—kids who might not have ever before experienced or might not continue to have families who care and encourage them. They may live in my house, but you become just as much a part of their family as I do while they are here.

WHAT IS FOSTER CARE?

Make no mistake, before I became a leading expert in foster care, and even before I was a foster parent, I had many misconceptions about what foster care really was, as well as about the children who were placed in it. I fell in line with believing many of the myths and stereotypes about foster care. It was only after I began training to be a foster parent that my eyes were opened, and I began to understand how the system worked and why it was sadly necessary. I say sadly necessary because I would love to live in a world where foster care was not necessary, where there was no need, where every child lived with their family and all were free from harm. Yet we live in a fallen world where Satan does prowl, and a world where children are abused, neglected, and abandoned.

In order for us to answer this call to care for His children in need and to work in the mission field that surrounds us, we need to better understand how foster care works and what it is all about. Let's examine what I wrote in the book, *The Foster Parenting Manual: A Practical Guide to Creating a Loving, Safe, and Stable Home.*

Foster care is a form of placement for children who are in need of being placed in a home or environment outside of their home of origin. On any given day in America, there are roughly 500,000 children in the foster care system. This placement is a twenty-four-hour substitute care for these children, while they are placed outside their own home. A child is often placed into foster care when a state's child protection agency determines that the home the child is living in is no longer a safe environment. After this determination has been made by a state, a judge must agree, signing all necessary paperwork in order for a child to be removed and placed into foster care, accordingly. During the time a foster child is placed in a foster home, the birth family is assigned a case plan. Each case plan is different, according to the challenges that the family faces, according to the reasons the child is placed into foster care. It is the goal of each case plan for a foster child to be reunited with the birth family or family members. This reunification occurs when the family has concluded the obligations of their case plan. Many courts allow a family one year to conclude the case plan. If a family is unable to meet the demands expected of them in the case plan after a court appointed time, the family may lose their permanent custody of the child.

As foster care is intended to be a temporary placement, the time frame in a foster home varies from one foster child to the next, with some staying only one day and others staying as long as a couple of years. The average amount of time a foster child spends in the foster care system is 28.6 months in length, with half of all foster children being placed in another home for a year or more. As a result, most of these children have not experienced a stable or nurturing environment during their early, formative years. Again, the length of time spent in a foster home is different for each child, dependent upon the child's situation. As a foster parent, you may never really know how long a foster child will stay in your house. A foster child may stay in your house for a day or for a year. One of the emotional challenges you will face as a foster parent is the uncertainty of the placement, and at times, the sad timing of a reunification with a foster child's birth family.

WHO ARE FOSTER CHILDREN?

Like so much of society, I had misconceptions about why a child might be in foster care. Growing up, I had heard whispers that "those foster kids" were somehow at fault, were often "bad kids" and were "trouble makers." Now, as I have had the privilege of caring for more than forty-five children in my home, I can boldly assure you that these children are not at fault. Instead, they are victims. They are victims from abuse and from neglect. They are children who want to lead a normal life, who want to play and laugh with other children their age, and who simply want someone to love them.

Foster care is available for any child between the ages of birth until eighteen years of age. When a child reaches the age of eighteen, most will exit the foster system. The average age of a child in custody is 10.2 years. Of all children in foster care, 47 percent of these are in their teens. When a child is placed in custody under foster care, and into your foster home, the intention is for the child to eventually be reunited with his/her birth family. Roughly six out of every ten children placed in foster care are reunited with birth parents or family members.

Children are placed under foster care for a number of reasons. Many of these reasons overlap, with the child suffering from numerous mental and emotional challenges. These reasons may include one or more of the following:

- **NEGLECT**: A child may be neglected in a number of ways. A parent may neglect a child's basic need for food, sanitary living conditions, proper medical care, and supervision. Finally, many foster children also suffer from emotional neglect, as a parent or adult does not meet their emotional needs.

- **PHYSICAL ABUSE**: Abuse takes many forms. One of these is the abuse through a physical injury caused by a parent or caregiver, with the severity of the injury sustained ranging from visible bruising to a more tragic signs of assault. Physical abuse can even take the form of locking a child in a closet or other confined space. Many times, the child welfare agency works with the parents in an attempt to help them learn alternate methods of discipline. Yet when these methods fail and a child becomes abused, the state steps in, and removes the child from the household.

- **SEXUAL ABUSE**: Sexual abuse also takes different forms, including voyeurism, the viewing of pornographic material or sexual acts with a child, or the act of sexual fondling, penetration, or rape of a child.

- **PARENTAL DRUG/ALCOHOL ABUSE**: Parental abuse of drugs and/or alcohol may result in neglect, physical abuse, or domestic violence.

- **CHILD DRUG/ALCOHOL ABUSE**: Parents may intentionally allow their children to take drugs and/or alcohol or may either ignore or be unaware of the child's abuse of drugs/alcohol.

- **DOMESTIC VIOLENCE**: When caretakers are engaged in violent altercations.

- **INADEQUATE HOUSING**: When a parent is no longer able to provide a clean, safe, healthy environment for a child. Many times, these children are homeless.

- **INCARCERATION**: When all parents, family members, and caregivers are unavailable due to their placement into prison or jail.

- **DEATH**: On very rare occasions, the death of one or both parents leads to a situation where there are no family members willing, able, or available to provide and care for a child.

- **ABANDONMENT**: Abandonment occurs when a parent or caregiver chooses to leave the child voluntarily. Many times, this abandonment may occur with a friend, neighbor, or a babysitter. Other times, a parent may simply leave the child at home for extended periods of time.

There are a number of reasons why a child might be placed into foster care. For some, they might live with foster parents unrelated to them. Other children may be placed with relatives for a temporary period of time. Finally, some children may live or reside in a group home setting, while those who need more intensive treatment may be placed in Treatment Foster Care, which provides therapeutic treatment services. The reunification between a child and his birth parents is always the end goal of foster care. Tragically, this does not always take place, leaving many children in foster care open for adoption every year.

As we know, our loving God calls all of His children to care for those in need. There are amazing ways God can use the church to help both foster children and foster parents. Perhaps the most important way we can help children in foster care is through the power of prayer. You see, these children face danger, darkness, tragedy, and trauma on a daily basis. Thousands of children in foster care need you and me to pray for them each day. Prayer ministries, or prayer teams, can be instrumental in helping members of a church become more involved in not only helping foster children but in changing the course of their lives.

Perhaps there is a church in your area looking for a way to minister to others. Maybe your own church is seeking ways to reach out to those in need. Hosting a local foster parent association and support group is one such way a church can serve foster parents. Another way is serving as a location for family visitations. Churches can provide a safe, consistent, warm, and inviting atmosphere for children and birth family members to meet. Not only can this be a form of outreach for a church, but the message of God's love and forgiveness is also being practiced.

As a church, as a nonprofit faith-based organization, and as God's people, we have the opportunity to be witnesses of God's great love for children in foster care, as well as His redeeming grace, mercy, and forgiveness. We can share our faith with these children and be His arms and legs working for His glory to help those in need. Our mission is clear. Let us now take this mission onto the mission field. Let us begin to care for the 500,000 children in foster care in not only our nation but in our states and in our own backyards.

QUESTIONS FOR DISCUSSION

Before you started reading this book, what was your opinion of foster children? What was your opinion of foster parents?

Before you started reading this book, what was your opinion of foster parents?

Do you know of any children in foster care in your own city?

How many children are in the foster care system in the United States on any given day?

What are some reasons why children are placed into foster care?

What does abuse look like to you?

Do you know of any children who have been abused, neglected, or abandoned?

Why is foster care a mission field?

What can you do, right now, as a child of God, to help His children in need?

The Dangers Children in Foster Care Face

I t is a different world, today. Our children are at danger from so many risks and from so many directions. Yet so many in our society are unfamiliar with these dangers. From human trafficking to online technology and social media to the opioid crisis that is gripping America, children in foster care are especially vulnerable and are at great risk. Let's examine these dangers.

Human Trafficking[1]

Modern-day slavery exists for children in the United States.

Children sold hour after hour, day after day, week after week, mostly for reasons of sex. Right here, in the land of the free, and the home of the brave. Children just like the ones who live in your home. Children just like the ones you are related to. Children just like the ones who live in your neighborhood.

In the first few days of February 2017 alone, several arrests of child sex traffickers were reported. In California, more than 470 people were arrested over a three-day period as the state's Operation Reclaim and Rebuild rescued dozens of children, many of them taken from the foster care system in some way. Twenty-two more were arrested in Detroit, Michigan, this time at the North American International Auto Show, as police rescued two more young children, under the age of sixteen. In Dallas, Texas, during the same month, a fifteen-year-old girl was rescued from a child sex trafficker. Another sixteen-year-old girl, also from Texas, was a victim of child sex trafficking. Police arrested an individual in Tulsa, Oklahoma, this time rescuing three minors from child sex trafficking.

Modern day slavery does exist. Right here, in America.

Yet, so many refuse to acknowledge it. So many in our society turn away.

Why is this?

Child sex trafficking makes us feel uncomfortable. It is not something we want to discuss, as the realities of it are heart wrenching, are disturbing, are tragic. Yet, child sex trafficking is happening, today, all around us. It is in our cities, and even in our neighborhoods. And it is happening to our children, with the average age of a child being trafficked at only twelve years old.

Senator Amy Klobuchar, Democrat from Minnesota, put it wisely when she said, "They're not even old enough to go to a prom, not even old enough to get a driver's license, and yet we still are seeing more and more of it on the Internet." The number of children being contacted by sexual predators online is disturbing and astounding at the same time. Approximately one out of every seven children is sexually contacted, or solicited, by a predator while online. Furthermore, many of these children are seriously pursued online by these predators, singling out these children in an attempt to lure them in.

Some reports indicate 300,000 children in the United States alone are prostituted each year. You shake your head in disbelief. I understand, the number is disturbing, to say the least. Furthermore, 2 million children are victims of child sex trafficking each year across the globe. The number is staggering, and hard to believe. Yet, the numbers are true, and society as a whole seems to look the other way.

Across the globe, human trafficking is a $32 billion industry each year and is on the rise in the United States. In one 2014 study by the Urban Institute in Atlanta, Georgia, some child traffickers in Atlanta make more than $32,000 a week. Furthermore, the same study also cited research discovering that Atlanta's illegal sex industry generates around $290 million a year.

Most youth who fall victim to prostitution today come from environments where they have already been sexually abused. To be sure, the majority of children in America who are exploited sexually have already endured a life of physical, sexual, or psychological abuse. Indeed, the contributor to a child entering into a life of child sex trafficking is a prior life of sexual abuse. Along with this, many of these children who have already been exposed to sexual abuse have problems with low self-esteem and do not receive the educational opportunities they deserve. For some teens who have suffered abuse from the hands of family members, they may seek escape by running away from home. As a result, they are more likely to end up homeless and may choose a lifestyle of prostitution in order to "make ends meet," financially, so to speak. These youth are more inclined to be placed into foster homes or group homes and are also more likely to run away. Pimps also attract children by targeting them in group homes, promising them gifts, a sense of belonging, and a place where they will be loved, as well as encouraging them with presents and gifts, all while grooming them for a life of prostitution.[2]

Children in foster care are especially vulnerable victims to sexual predators. Through their past history of abuse and neglect, these children experience higher levels of anxiety than children from traditional homes.

Perhaps the type of anxiety foster children face the most is separation anxiety, an excessive concern that they might be separated from their home, family, and those they are attached to the most. Sadly so many youth in foster care are moved from one home to the next, known as multiple displacement. The more a child is moved from home to home, the larger their anxieties grow and the bigger their concern becomes. In an attempt to try to protect themselves, these children often create walls to separate themselves and not let others into their lives. Others feel starved for a sense of family and belonging. However it manifests itself, this type of anxiety and insecurity can make them vulnerable to sexual predators as they search for love. For those foster children who have been abused in some way in the past, they may be more likely to show inappropriate sexual behavior or seek out love in inappropriate places.

For many children in foster care, their personal search for love ends in sexual exploitation. With no one to show them early in their lives what true unconditional or healthy loving relationships are, children in foster care often cannot recognize manipulative behavior.

Today's sexual predators recognize that children in foster care are especially vulnerable to this kind of assault.

Scripture is specific about those who might hurt innocent children. It warns us that those who harm children will face judgment: "It would be better for him if a millstone were hung around his neck and he were cast into the sea than that he should cause one of these little ones to sin" (Luke 17:2).

DANGERS OF ONLINE TECHNOLOGY

Curtis was not in control. In fact, he had no control with just about anything in his life. After all, Curtis was in foster care.

Thirteen-year-old Curtis was placed into foster care after suffering neglect from a mother who was addicted to and sold illegal drugs. He had been separated from his other two siblings, a younger brother and sister, as there were no foster homes in the area able to take in three children at that time. His father had been in and out of the family's life, just as he had been in and out of jail. When Curtis arrived in his new foster home, he was confused, he was lonely, and he was scared. Curtis had been taken from everything he knew. He had been taken from his mother, his father, his brother, and his sister. He had been taken from his bedroom, his toys, his baseball card collection, his pet dog, his house, his home. The teen had been taken from his grandparents, his aunts, his uncles, his cousins, his neighbors, his friends, his teachers, and his classmates. Curtis had been taken from everything that was familiar to him, everything he knew, and everything he loved.

Against his wishes, Curtis was thrust into a strange home with strange people and strange rules. The teenager had no control over the situation, had no say in where he was going to live, and had no power in when or if he one day return home to his mother and family. But he had control over one thing—his online life. The foster teen was able to create an online identity, one he could control and one he could escape into. During the day, Curtis was reminded he was a foster child at every possible moment. Whether it was at his new school, with his new teachers and fellow students, to living with foster parents and his foster brother, Curtis was unable to escape his unwanted status of being in a foster home and a child of foster care.

In the evenings, though, Curtis could escape behind his computer and find refuge from his fears and anxieties. Through social networking, playing online games, and texting his friends, Curtis felt like he was in charge of his own actions. This was the only thing the foster teen had control of, and he was not about to let it go.

Cyberbullying[3] is the platform in which the twenty-first century bully uses to inflict pain and humiliation upon another. Cyberbullying is the use of technology to embarrass, threaten, tease, harass, or even target another person. With the use of online technology and social networking sites, today's bully can follow their targeted victim wherever the child may go. Whether the child is in school, at the park, at the movie theater, or at home, whenever that child has a cell phone or access to online technology, he can be bullied. In essence, this form of bullying can be nonstop, twenty-four hours a day, seven days a week.

The number of children who have been exposed to some sort of cyberbullying is astounding. According to McAfee, which is part of Intel Security, 87 percent of today's youth have witnessed cyberbullying. The Cyberbullying Research Center found that 33 percent of students have acknowledged that they have experienced cyberbullying themselves.

Cyberbullying takes many forms. Indeed, as today's youth are so very technologically savvy, they can use this technology as a tool to bully others. This type of bullying can be done through emails, chat rooms, social networking sites, text messages, cell phones, and even websites. There are countless ways a child can be bullied with this type of technology, and the number of ways is increasing, just as technology continues to advance.

Tragically, cyberbullying also leads to suicide. The Center for Disease Control and Prevention (CDC) found that suicide is the third leading cause of death among young people. Shockingly, roughly 4,400 young people commit suicide in the United States each year. The CDC estimates that there are at least one hundred suicide attempts for every suicide committed among young people. Children like fourteen-year-old Ryan Halligan and thirteen-year-old Megan Meier who both hung themselves in an attempt to escape from cyberbullying, eighteen-year-old Jessica Logan and thirteen-year-old Hope Sitwell who also hung themselves after enduring the horrors of sexting, and fifteen-year-old Amanda Todd who hung herself after being both bullied and blackmailed online; these stories are sadly all too common.

Now, don't get me wrong. There are wonderful benefits of online technology and social media. I use it daily for a variety of reasons. It offers me the amazing opportunity to connect, converse with, and help thousands of foster and adoptive parents from across the globe. When I travel from one foster care conference in one state to speaking at a church in another state to delivering a key note speech in yet another, I am able to stay in touch and communicate with my children and family through online technology and social media. I can listen to music, watch movies, and even do research, all through social media and online technology.

Yet, for all the benefits online technology and social networking provide, the dangers and horrors are almost overwhelming. And foster children are especially susceptible to many of these dangers. As more foster children turn to online technology and social networking for entertainment, communication, and escape, the number of foster children that are being placed in harm's way is increasing. Unfortunately, this is one area many foster parents, and child welfare workers for that matter, do not recognize or are unfamiliar with. It is vital for those who work with foster children to be aware of these dangers in order to be better equipped to protect the children in their care.

THE OPIOID CRISIS[4]

America is in the midst of a deadly crisis that is killing people by the thousands.

The opioid epidemic in the United States claimed more than 33,000 deaths in 2015, as public health officials call it the worst drug crisis in the nation's history. Indeed, the deaths from heroin alone have surged and have claimed more lives in 2015 than homicides by guns. These drugs, these opioids, are used to often block out pain. Whether illegal, such as heroin, or prescribed by doctors yet are also finding their way on to the black market, such as Vicodin and OxyContin, the rise in opioid use in America is both dramatic and disturbing.

Yet, perhaps more disturbing is the number of children being affected by the increase of opioid use in all fifty states. The images of parents passed out in cars from drugs while their children are sitting in back seats have gone viral through social media. The video of a two-year-old toddler in a store trying to wake up her mother who had passed out from an overdose, has also been seen by millions online.

As more and more parents become addicted to opioids, thousands of more children are being placed into a foster care system throughout the nation, a system that is struggling to properly assist these children due to lack of resources, foster parents, and funding. According to Vermont Governor Peter Shumlin, "All of those involved in the child protection system are doing heroic work, but they need additional resources."

The larger number of children being placed into foster care, nationwide, is due much in part of an increase in parental drug usage and substance abuse, with heroin use being the chief drug increasing among parents. Other substance abuse among parents include meth, cocaine, and prescription medication abuse.

As the opioid crisis in America continues to climb, continues to claim more victims, and continues to lead to more deaths, it is the children in the nation that are falling through the cracks. It is the children in the nation that are the hidden victims. It is the children in the nation that are unable to protect themselves from this drug use.

Sadly, heroin has made a comeback as a major drug of choice. "The heroin epidemic is forcing more kids into foster care, but in most states, funding can't keep up with the need," according to Lana Freeman and the National Foster Parent Association. "The states need more foster families, the workers need more resources, and parents need more services."

With the increase in children being placed into foster care, the foster care system is struggling to keep up. With roughly 450,000 children in foster care across the nation, there are not enough foster homes, as foster care agencies face the challenge of recruitment and retention of foster parents. The end result is simply that there are not enough homes for children in need to be placed in, or a child is moved from one home to another.[5]

Yet, what is perhaps the saddest and most heartbreaking is when babies suffer. Like one I recently saw in the hospital. The baby lay screaming in the hospital crib, its tiny frame racked with pain.

Powerless to help, the nurse tried to comfort the baby as best she could. Two more babies in the hospital were suffering with the same condition, yet there was little she could do.

The newborn baby was going through withdrawal from drugs—drugs transmitted by her mother during pregnancy. Known as neonatal abstinence syndrome, or NAS, these withdrawal symptoms can take the form of seizures, elevated heart and respiratory rate, difficulty in sleeping and eating, extreme bouts of irritability, and even problems in growth development.

As America is in the grips of an opioid epidemic, the number of babies born dependent on heroin and other opiates continues to climb as well.

Indeed, the number of children born with neonatal abstinence syndrome has quadrupled over the course of fifteen years in the United States. Shockingly, up to 94 percent of babies born to mothers who used opioids while pregnant will suffer symptoms of drug withdrawal. Maine, Vermont, and West Virginia lead the nation. Out of every one thousand babies born in these states, at least thirty are born with NAS. Another study found that babies born the past decade suffering from NAS increased five-fold across the nation. Furthermore, yet another study found that a baby is born suffering from opiate withdrawals every twenty-five minutes.

I have seen it firsthand. I have held many a baby in my own arms as they suffered with withdrawal, as they screamed in pain. Some have become permanent family members.[6] Yes, the three I had adopted from foster care have all come from mothers addicted to drugs while pregnant. All three of these children face challenges because of this.

Broken families, lost children, and a foster care system that cannot meet the increasing demand cannot keep up with this nationwide crisis. It is up to people of faith to truly help these children and their families.

QUESTIONS FOR DISCUSSION

What did you find shocking or disturbing about the issue of child sex trafficking in America?

Are you aware of any child sex trafficking stories in your city?

How do children from foster care fall victim to child sex trafficking?

How can your church or faith-based organization help to prevent child sex trafficking in your city?

What does God say about placing children in danger or harm in Matthew 18:6?

What are some of the biggest dangers youth in foster care face with online technology?

Who can be a victim of online technology dangers?

Why is the opioid crisis spreading and becoming more of a troubling problem?

How is today's church or people of faith helping protect children from these dangers?

THE ROLE OF THE CHURCH

A. B.'s STORY

———o———

This is what it looks like for a church to support foster care. It looks like seeing the need for a play set and organizing the efforts to purchase and assemble it. It looks like dropping off dinner on the first night of a new placement. It's volunteering to tutor a foster kid, donating clothes, or paying for a kid to go to camp. It looks like dropping off toys and clothes when a foster family takes a child out of their typical age range or setting up and paying for their house to be cleaned when things are tough. It looks like bringing groceries after an injury and being Santa for children in foster care.

It's a young adult forming a bond with a child and occasionally taking them for some one-on-one time or a senior adult telling you to come use their pool. It looks like going through a background check so you can babysit or help transport a child to therapy appointments. It's providing respite care. It's donating furniture to set up a home when the kids get to go back home to mom. It looks like a Chick-fil-A gift card or an offer to pray for you.

It's providing meeting space and childcare rooms for monthly foster parent trainings. It looks like helping entertain and love on kids while a foster mom fixes four plates at Wednesday night supper. It looks like a hug, an understanding smile, a word of encouragement, and lots of prayer. It looks like love. It looks like our family at First Baptist Church Statesboro.

So many times, I am asked how do I do it. How do I care for up to eleven children in my house at one time?

If it wasn't for members of my church, I am not sure I could be a foster parent today. From the tangible support to the prayers, the church I attend and belong to has played a critical role as my wife and I care for children in need in our own home. Indeed, there are times when I count on the members of my church to help us and to help the children.

As God's people, each of us has the opportunity to bring His love to both children in need and those who care for them, as well as help ease the burden foster parents face when caring for children in need in their homes. When a foster parent and a child from foster care comes to your church or faith-based institution, it is an amazing opportunity for ministry. Their time at your church might be the very first time they have ever entered a church at all. Or it may be the first time in a long time they have stepped foot into a church, as they may have been hurt in the past by people of faith. Their time in your church can be a time of healing, of beginning a new journey of faith, and of being introduced to God's love, His mercy, and His promise of eternal life.

As we know, God does call all of His children to care for those in need and gives us all individual talents and abilities to do so. There are amazing ways God can use the church to help both foster children and foster parents. Do you remember Rhonda Sciortino? She wrote the beautiful and powerful introduction to my book *Faith and Foster Care: How We Impact God's Kingdom*. Recently, I had a conversation with her, and this is what she told me:

> *Many people hear, "the church and foster care," and immediately think, "Oh no, I don't need to pay attention to that because I'm not going to foster or adopt." For too many years, the main focus of connecting the*

church to foster kids was to recruit foster or adoptive parents. If that doesn't happen to be God's call on your life, there was no place for you.

As a former foster kid, I am the first one to say that not everyone is supposed to foster or adopt. But the big detail everyone seems to overlook is that everyone can do something! When people in the faith community engage their skills, talents, and abilities to help kids and families, the lives of everyone involved are enriched.

The hurting people in our own communities are the next mission field for the church. There are children who are being neglected, abused, and trafficked within fifteen minutes of you, right now. There are people who have gone days without a decent meal, there are people who haven't slept in a bed for weeks, there are people who have lost their hope and feel it would be easier to die than to try again. People of faith can eradicate social isolation and the societal ills that accompany it simply by getting up out of pew and walking out into the streets. It can be done. One way to do this is through the Love Is Action Community Initiative, which gives every person, business, and group some way to safely engage with others. For information on bringing LIA to your community, go to www.loveisactioncommunityinitiative.org.

—Rhonda Sciortino, chairperson, Successful Survivors Foundation, and author of *Successful Survivors: The Eight Character Traits of Survivors and How You Can Attain Them*

As a foster and adoptive parent, I need your prayers. My children from foster care living in my home need your prayers also. The power of prayer is strong, and it gives me strength as I care for His children in need. As I travel across the nation, I hear the same belief echoed from thousands of foster and adoptive parents. Prayer—consistent, fervent prayer—is one of the most powerful ways a church can help children in need and those who care for them.

As I share in my book *Faith and Foster Care*, "Children in foster care face danger, darkness, tragedy, and trauma on a daily basis. These children are caught up in what I believe to be a spiritual war, as they come under attack from so many different angles. They need people on their side, lifting them up in prayer each day, from the time the sun comes up to the time they go to bed. Prayer ministries, or prayer teams, can be instrumental in helping members of a church become more involved in not only helping foster children, but in changing the course of their lives. Without a doubt, God hears our prayers and answers them in His way.

"There are a number of ways a church can pray for a foster child and his foster family . . . A prayer team can also begin praying for the child even before he is placed into his foster home, praying that the transition is as smooth and as comfortable as possible. Prayer teams can pray for the specific needs of the child and for any obstacles or hurdles that he might have in front of him. Along with these requests, church members can also keep the foster family lifted up in prayer as well, at all times asking that God grant them the strength, wisdom, and compassion they need as they minister to their foster child."

I have witnessed the power of prayer at work in my family, in the children in my home, and in the lives of many of the birth parents of these children. When we pray according to God's will, we are opening up a power that is unstoppable. Jesus told us this Himself when He said, "If you remain in me and my words remain in you, ask whatever you wish, and it will be done for you" (John 15:7).

CHELSEA'S STORY

My husband and I were going through training to become foster parents and were becoming discouraged with the level of information we were receiving, particularly regarding the kinds of trauma we should expect to encounter. We were both beginning to wonder if we would be able to handle a foster child's behavior. We decided to keep going, reluctantly.

One Wednesday morning, I sat down and put pencil to paper to figure up what all we needed to purchase in order to outfit the foster children's new room—bunk beds, dressers, curtains, etc. I came up with around $2,000. At this point, I reached the realization that we may not be able to provide what we needed for the children. My husband was at work, so I decided to relay my fears to him that evening after we had tucked our two kids in to bed.

That evening at church, a widower gave us a card sealed in an envelope. His son was soon to be married, so we assumed it was a wedding shower invitation. I got in my car after church and opened the envelope. His enclosed note stated how much he loved our family and how encouraged he was by getting to see us every Sunday and Wednesday. He stated that God richly blesses him and his company he owns, and he felt called to share some of his blessings with us. He begged us to take the enclosed check, as it wasn't from him, but from God. Enclosed was a check for $2,000.

I broke down crying immediately. My husband was in a separate car, and I called him immediately to read him the note and tell him how much money the gentleman had given us. He started crying as well when I told him how much money we needed to outfit our new children's bedrooms. Up to that point, I was the only person who knew how much we needed to finish preparing our home in order to care for children in foster care and to be foster parents. Our prayers had been answered. The power of prayer had worked.

We had no doubt the money was truly from God, and we gratefully accepted it, along with the knowledge that God was telling us in the most obvious way possible that our future involved fostering children. We went on to foster seven kids and adopted two of those kids before closing our home. Our house and our family were full.

There are a number of ways we can pray for our foster children. Let's look at how we can do this from my book *Faith and Foster Care:*

"We need to become prayer warriors for our foster children, lifting them up in prayer on a daily basis. Not only should we pray for the children, but our foster children's caseworkers also need prayer. After all, their job is a difficult one, and they have emotional ties to the children as well. Just today I spoke with a caseworker who told me she worked with a child for over two years who was placed back into a birth parent's home, despite the caseworker's pleas. With tears forming in her eyes, this caseworker told me that the concerns she had about the child's reunification with the parents came true, and that she continues to pray for the child each day.

"Furthermore, the birth parents of the children are also in need of prayer. Despite the abuse, neglect, and other challenges and horrors the biological parents and birth family members may have placed upon these children, they are children of God, just as you and I are. This calling might be difficult, though. Are we praying for the well being and healing of the birth parent or for the family to spend more time in jail? Are we praying that the children be reunified with their biological family or that the parent's rights to the child are terminated so we can adopt the child? You may be the only one praying for these parents. We need to put aside our personal judgment and beliefs and instead pray that God's healing hand would move and His will be done for all involved. As Christians, we are called to pray for mercy and justice, for not just the children but for their parents too. These parents may be victims of abuse, neglect, rape, and violence also. To be honest with you, I remind myself some times that I need to walk humbly with our God, that I am a sinner just like anyone else, and that I am no better than those who would hurt their child, my foster child. We all need to keep the words of Micah 6:8 in or hearts when we pray for our foster child's family members. The words of this Scripture verse are both beautiful and powerful reminders of this directive. 'He has shown you, O mortal, what is good. And what does the LORD require of you? To act justly and to love mercy and to walk humbly with your God.'"

I continue in *Faith and Foster Care* by sharing ways foster parents can pray each day. I believe they also apply to all Christians. It is worth repeating, and it is important I share it again. This time, let's examine these points of prayer as a mission for today's church and faith-based organizations.

1. We can pray for the children who are coming into foster care right at this very moment. Pray that these children in need are placed with loving, supportive foster families who are able to meet each child's specific needs. Pray for these children in need as they face the emotionally confusing and traumatic experience of being taken from their family members and being placed in a new home.

2. We can pray that children in foster care do not experience multiple disruptions or move from foster home to foster home to foster home. Each time a child is moved from one home to another, it is a time of trauma and loss. The lack of stability in a home environment is incredibly difficult and challenging on so many levels. Pray that the child is placed in a home that will provide the structure, stability, resources, and love that he so dearly needs, and that he remain in this home until he is able to reunify with his parents, find an adoptive family, or be placed into his forever home.

3. *We can pray that the children remain in foster care for as short a time as it is safely possible. The more time a child remains in care, the more likely it is that he will not find his forever home and a loving family that will care for him. Pray that God prepares the hearts and home a loving forever family for him if his parental rights are terminated.*

4. *We can pray that the child is able to form a healthy relationship with his caseworker and that the caseworker is one that is loving, kind, compassionate, and understanding to his needs.*

5. *We can pray that if the child has siblings in other foster homes, they are all able to stay in contact with each other. Pray that, if it is possible and healthy, the siblings are able to remain in a foster home together.*

6. *We can pray that God heals the trauma, pain, and profound damage to which these children have been exposed. Pray that God will also protect them from any other dangers or threats that they might face in their lives.*

7. *We can pray that the judge, caseworkers, and those who decide the child's fate receive the wisdom they need in order to make the best decision that is in the child's best interest. If parental rights should be terminated, pray this action is done as painlessly as possible for all involved.*

8. *We can pray for teens who have aged out of the foster care system. Pray they do not experience the dangers and horrors that often await them, like homelessness, incarceration, drug usage, prostitution, unemployment, and other threats. Pray that they find a loving Christian family that will look after them, care for them, and mentor them, in both good times and bad. Pray that they find Jesus Christ as their Savior and develop a personal relationship with Him.*

9. *We can pray that we as foster parents can be the hands, feet, voice, and heart of our loving God. Pray that we are able share with these children in our care the fruit of the Spirit that God has blessed each of us with.*

10. We can pray for the biological children of our foster parents, that they are instruments of God's love, and that their hearts are open to their fellow foster sibling.

11. We can pray that more people would choose to follow the path of becoming foster parents. With hundreds of thousands of children in foster care and so few foster parents, the need is strong, yet so few are willing to pick up this cross of service.

12. We can pray for the birth parents and biological family members. Pray that they find the strength they need to overcome their personal demons, such as drugs and alcohol addiction, incarceration, unemployment, mental illness, or other challenges they face. Pray that they receive the resources, programs, and help they need. Pray that they are able to make a full and complete recovery so that they can be loving parents, allowing for a safe and healthy reunification with their children. Pray that they also come to know Christ as their Savior.

13. We can pray for the social workers. Pray that they find the wisdom when placing a child into the right home, a home that is best suited for both the child and the family. Pray that they receive the strength they need with the many difficult aspects of their jobs. Pray that they receive the compassion and love they need to share with both the children and their biological family members.

14. We can pray that social workers receive the funding and resources they need from the state. Pray that they also find joy and satisfaction in their job and that they rely upon God.

15. We can pray that the lawmakers in each state make decisions that are best for the children, as well as for the foster parents. Pray that these lawmakers and politicians have their eyes and hearts open to the realities that children in foster care face, as well as the challenges and frustrations that foster parents and caseworkers face. Pray that our lawmakers turn to God for His wisdom in these decisions.

16. We can pray that our churches hear the call to help children in foster care, and that they answer this call from God with grace and mercy. Pray that our churches and church leaders are equipped with the resources and support that is needed for this mission field and that they make an immediate impact in the lives of foster children, and in foster care in general.

DEANNA'S STORY

I work for a state child protection agency as a resource coordinator. My job is to recruit and retain foster parents. In order to do that, I also search for resources for those foster parents. As a state-run agency, we do not pay well, and while I know foster parents are not necessarily caring for children from foster care for the money, they are also not in it to go broke either! When I started with the State of Vermont, we had a connection with churches in our district under the heading of PINS, which stands for People in Need of Services. It was a well-managed program, and we had formal arrangements with the churches in our area. In the nature of working for the government, this program was cut during budget cuts. I have stayed connected with those original churches and have reached out to other churches in my district as well.

There is a one church in my area that provides holiday gifts for all the children we are working with who are not in state custody. This church provides one practical gift such as clothing, hats and mittens, boots, etc. and one fun gift for the child depending on their likes and dislikes. The social workers give the families a form with questions about interests, authors they like to read, music they enjoy listening to, and clothing needs and sizes. Church members pick a form, and they fulfill the child's wishes (within reason, of course).

Every child who is in state custody receives a backpack and school supplies to start the school year. These packs and supplies used to be provided solely by our churches, but our caseloads have exploded due to the opiate problem in our state, so we have reached out to other civic organizations to help with this project. Yet it is the churches in our area that, time after time, take on the bulk of the needs. They start early in the summer gathering donations and then put the bags together and deliver them to our office. The bags come packed with pens, pencils, notebooks, rulers, etc., all donated by the church members.

We have a once-a-year $100 activity fee each family can access for any child in custody, but as you can imagine, $100 does not go very far! If a child has a need for money in order to participate in a sport, horseback riding lessons, dance lessons, or other activity, I will reach out to our partners in the faith-based community and explain what the child is hoping to do. So many times, the churches will donate to that need. I even had a church that paid twice weekly for horseback riding lessons for an autistic child in foster care. Now, years later, that child continues to love horses, and the church continues to help with some of his expenses. If a child wants to attend camp, and between our activity fee and scholarships we happen to come up short for the cost, I will reach out to the churches and get donations.

Recently, I sent letters to all the churches in my district and offered to come speak to the congregations about fostering. So far, I have been asked to speak four different times! In my own neighborhood, there is a universal church group who called me and essentially interviewed me over the phone. A few weeks later, I received a letter from them with a check. The letter said the money was to be used for pack and plays, diapers, wipes, and other items for parents not entirely ready to take on a baby. The note said the person who interviewed me spoke to the church, and they dedicated their collection to our office.

QUESTIONS FOR DISCUSSION

How is prayer a form of communication with God?

What does the verse 1 Thessalonians 5:17 truly mean to you?

How have you seen prayer work in your life?

Why should we pray for children in foster care?

For the child who is being abused today, how does prayer help that child?

Why do foster parents need people to pray for them?

Birth parents and biological family members have often brought great pain, abuse, and trauma to children in foster care. Do they deserve your prayers?

How can your church or faith-based organization create a prayer team or group to prayer for the foster care community in your own area?

SERVING CHILDREN
IN FOSTER CARE

*T*here are many ways churches, corporately, can support the foster care community in their area. Nearly any size church can play a role in advocating for foster families, and this chapter covers a few of those possibilities.

SAFE HAVENS

My plane trip to Texas was canceled, leaving me standing in the terminal, alongside dozens of others, stranded without a flight. As I was scheduled to speak to a group of foster parents at a convention, I was anxious, and even a little stressed. This was the second time in a month I had encountered flight troubles. Just weeks before, I was stranded in Chicago, Illinois, snowed in and missing a flight to Iowa for a speaking engagement at their state conference.

Refusing to miss the seminar I was presenting on the dangers of online technology and social networking that foster children face, I rented a car, driving the additional hours and miles. Not only had I been looking forward to working with the caseworkers and foster parents of that area of Texas, I simply did not want to let people down. After all, I was scheduled to attend, made a commitment to do so, and it was my responsibility to see that I made it there. Fortunately, I was able to make it, held some exciting seminars over the next few days, and met some wonderful people, all dedicated to helping children in foster care.

Unfortunately, there are those times when schedules do not go as planned, and individuals are let down. For children in foster care, this can be especially difficult when it comes to visitations with birth parents and biological family members. As one who has watched many of my own foster children come home from disappointing visitations, my own heart has broken, as these children struggle to figure out why their mother or father did not come to see them.

For children in foster care, visitations with family members are often an event that they look forward to with great eagerness. After all, they are seeing their parents or other family members, being reunited with them, if only for a very brief time. Oftentimes, visitations are held at child welfare agencies, while other times they are held in neutral locations, such as restaurants, parks, and even faith-based institutions. The time usually flies by quickly, and the child and biological family member are once again separated until the next meeting. Visitations are important for a number of reasons and help to maintain the relationship between both child and adult.

Yet there are those times when a biological family member cannot make it, for whatever reason, and the scheduled visit is cancelled. [Many times, it may be due to the fact that the biological parents are intimidated by the foster care or child welfare agency's office, and find excuses not to attend.] Too many times, these children are left wondering why their parents did not show. Self-doubt sets in, as they question if it was something they may have done, or perhaps if their parents were mad at them. Some may believe their parents don't care about them, and that they do not even matter. For all involved, it is another rejection, another painful experience, and another heartbreak.[7]

Missy was a child from foster care who lived in our home for almost a year. The eight-year-old had been placed into foster care due to neglect and severe drug abuse by her mother. Missy would often misbehave in school the day after a visitation. Missy's mother had been coming down from Atlanta to meet with our foster daughter during visitation. She was regularly on drugs and had very little contact with her own mother. The child welfare agency's policy is that if suspected of being under the influence, a parent must have a drug check. There were occasions when Missy's mother either failed the test or simply did not show up for the visitations.

As I was often the one to pick her up on my way home from school each week, I was faced with the question of what to tell this young and confused girl why her mommy wasn't coming to see her. Too many times, I would walk into the agency's visitation room and find Missy staring out the window, waiting for her mother to visit, with tears streaming down her face. Each time, my own heart would be filled with sadness for this little girl who was torn away from the only family she knew and placed with us, strangers in a strange home. "Why didn't my mommy come?" Missy would ask me, between sobs.

"Sweetheart, maybe she's sick," I might answer one week. Another week, when faced with the same question, I would answer her with "Missy, maybe her car is not working." How could I explain to an eight-year-old girl that her mother failed a drug test or simply didn't show up? It wasn't fair to Missy, and she struggled greatly with this.

Visitations can be difficult for all involved. For the child, for the birth parents, and for the foster parents, visitations are often times of anxiety and stress. Yet they are necessary, mandatory, and often beneficial for families trying to heal. For many people, like Missy's biological mother, a child welfare office or building may seem threatening or intimidating, and meeting in these locations may be stressful to both the child and the family. The church can play a vital role by providing a safe, consistent, warm, and inviting atmosphere for children and birth family members to meet during visitation sessions. It is a form of outreach for a church and a way to exemplify Christ's love and forgiveness.

One way churches can facilitate visitation sessions is through the Safe Haven program, which trains volunteers to provide a safe, friendly, and stress-free environment. By doing so, the family can focus their attention and energy on the visitation itself as they seek to build and maintain a positive relationship in an environment that helps promote healing for both the child and the adult—healing that is essential for both.

Both foster parents and biological family members are given different times of arrival and departure. In some churches where Safe Havens are located, foster parents drop off their child and spend their free time shopping, running errands, or even having a bite to eat by themselves. Shortly afterward, as the child is playing with trained volunteers, the birth parents arrive and spend time with the child. Volunteers are trained to observe and ensure the children are safe and that the biological family members act in an appropriate manner.

For a number of years, I used a Safe Haven location at a local church for visitations between my own children from foster care and their birth families. The visitations were held in several of the church nurseries, where both child and parent could play together. During the course of those visits, I noticed over and over that the children were much happier and at peace with visits at the Safe Haven than they were at the local child welfare agency.

Let's look at what one foster parent had to say about the visitations at a church in her area.

JENNIFER'S STORY

We got our foster license in August 2015. We decided to become foster parents because my biological children were getting older and were not home much. As my children were from a previous marriage, and my husband had never had children of his own, I wanted him to be able to experience raising children like I had years ago. Our first placement was a baby, who we picked up from the hospital shortly after he was born. Now, with infants in foster care, there are often more visitations with biological parents and birth family members, of course. In fact, we often have visitations up to three times a week and for two hours at a time.

Some of the visitations were at the home of the family members, where a transporter would take the baby, while others were held at a Methodist church, through their Safe Haven program. We really preferred visitations at the church with Safe Havens. The church was much cleaner, smelled fresh, and so many of the volunteers were so friendly to our little one.

FOOD MINISTRY

It is common for churches and people of faith to provide meals for new mothers, those who are elderly or sick, and grieving families. These are wonderfully helpful and caring ministries that provide a much-needed service. When foster parents have children placed into their homes and families, it can be a hectic and busy time. Add to that the sudden need for doctor, dentist, and optometrist appointments in an attempt at getting caught up with medical needs, along with court hearings, visitations, enrolling the child into a new school, and helping the child catch up academically, it is easy to see how a foster parent can quickly become overwhelmed and swamped with things to do. Add to that the challenge of having to cook for a house full of children night in and night out. As one who has lived this lifestyle many times, I can assure you that finding time to cook a healthy meal, or even any meal for that matter, can be yet another challenge.

On occasion, my wife and I have had the great blessing of having a weekly meal delivered to our house by a member of our church. Let me tell you something: A weekly meal goes a long way in helping a foster family. Whether it is in the first few days of a placement of a child in a foster home or even if the child has been with the family for some time, this is a great gift and ministry that a church can offer a family that has a great deal on its plate. Many times, the first month or so of a placement of a child is known as the "honeymoon phase." For many foster parents, the hard work begins after this phase. A food ministry to a foster family truly takes away the stress of having to prepare meals while taking care of all the other unique responsibilities, duties, and challenges foster families face each day.

Let's look at what a number of foster parents told me when I asked them how church and faith-based groups helped them with meals.

Aubrey's, Sarah's and Wendy's Stories

My husband and I felt led to foster after hearing of the foster care crisis in our county, state, and nation. That's when we learned about the organization, The Call, and that they had an information meeting coming up. The Call brings awareness for the need of foster/adoptive homes and works closely with DFCS to seek out and train families. (They have nothing to do with placing children in homes.) My personal experience with our local organization has been great. They have a clothing closet that has everything—clothes, diapers, cribs, books, wipes, shoes, and more—and foster families and DFCS have access to it 24/7. The closet also has a freezer and refrigerator stocked with freezer meals, fresh garden produce, and farm fresh eggs, among other things, all donated by our amazing community, Sunday school classes, and life groups. These meals are there for a family to grab when they need a break from cooking or are delivered when a family receives a new placement, a family member is sick, or just to show love and support. —Aubrey

Our foster daughter had a medical condition that required her to have major cranial surgery at five months. Our small group generously gave our family enough money to help cover the costs of hospital parking and meals while we stayed in the hospital for five days and nights. When we returned home, they provided meals for our family for a week and half. Such sweet blessings that helped us feel loved and cared for and helped ease some of the stress our family went through. —Sarah

Our church wraps its loving arms around foster parents in a very big way! We have a care team that brings meals once a week (we have been receiving dinner on Mondays for about four years). Our care team prays for our family and babysits our kids during court and other appointments. Our church also provides foster parenting trainings (with childcare) and IMPACT trainings, a clothing closet, diaper drives, Christmas gifts, and family fun days for the foster families in our church. We are truly blessed! —Wendy

Your Gifts and Your Talents

Our Heavenly Father has given each of us a special gift, a special talent. My talents are probably different from yours, and your talent is probably different from your friends and family, your fellow church members, and even your spouse. A talent is something given at birth, instinctually, and these talents give you unique skills and abilities. Scripture tells us each of us is born with distinct talents and gifts that set us apart from each other. When we discover the talents God has given us, we are better able to use them in order to give Him the glory and point others to our loving God. Let's look at what Scripture says about our talents.

> Do you see someone skilled in their work?
> They will serve before kings; they will not
> serve before officials of low rank.
> —Proverbs 22:29

> Now about the gifts of the Spirit, brothers and sisters,
> I do not want you to be uninformed. You know that when
> you were pagans, somehow or other you were influenced
> and led astray to mute idols. Therefore I want you to
> know that no one who is speaking by the Spirit of God says,
> "Jesus be cursed," and no one can say, "Jesus is Lord,"
> except by the Holy Spirit. There are different kinds of
> gifts, but the same Spirit distributes them. *There are
> different kinds of service, but the same Lord. There are
> different kinds of working, but in all of them and in everyone
> it is the same God at work.* Now to each one the
> manifestation of the Spirit is given for the common good.
> To one there is given through the Spirit a message of
> wisdom, to another a message of knowledge by means of the
> same Spirit, to another faith by the same Spirit, to another
> gifts of healing by that one Spirit, to another miraculous
> powers, to another prophecy, to another distinguishing
> between spirits, to another speaking in different kinds of
> tongues, and to still another the interpretation of
> tongues. All these are the work of one and the same Spirit,
> and he distributes them to each one, just as he determines.
> —1 Corinthians 12:1–11 (emphasis added)

For we are God's handiwork, created in Christ Jesus to do
good works, which God prepared in advance for us to do.
—Ephesians 2:10

Every good and perfect gift is from above,
coming down from the Father of the heavenly lights,
who does not change like shifting shadows.
—James 1:17

Each of you should use whatever gift you have received to
serve others, as faithful stewards of God's grace in its
various forms. If anyone speaks, they should do so as one
who speaks the very words of God. If anyone serves, they
should do so with the strength God provides, so that in
all things God may be praised through Jesus Christ. To him
be the glory and the power for ever and ever. Amen.
—1 Peter 4:10–11

Over the years, I have encountered people from all walks of life who are sharing their gifts and their talents with children from foster care, as well as the foster parents. Their stories continue to inspire me each day. I hope they not only inspire you but encourage you to think outside the box, so to speak, on how you can help both the children and the foster parents in your own way and with your own talents. Please allow me to share some of these stories with you.

Dan Parisi wanted to make a difference. A franchise owner of Sports Clips Haircuts, with stores in Massachusetts, Parisi felt children did not need to be nervous about having unkempt or messy hair when they go back to school. So he decided to do something about it by giving away free haircuts and providing "a service to the many children who don't get a quality haircut," Dan said. "It just felt like it was the right thing to do. There's all these kids that don't get to experience those kind of things, like a quality haircut." Dan's act of kindness to these children helps bring a sense of dignity and normalcy to them as well. Dan is also helping foster parents financially, as haircuts often come out of the personal cost to those foster parents that have children in care living with them.

"My first exposure to foster parenting was when I was about five years old," Dan told me. "My father had a friend who was a barber. We would go to the barber's house for my haircuts. We would walk in, and he would bring out a barber's chair into his kitchen. There was always a house full of children of all ages. I did not know until I was probably about ten or eleven years old that the barber and his wife were foster parents. I remember him and my father talking when I was getting my haircut and the barber talking about the latest child they 'took in' and learning later from my father about foster parenting.

"One afternoon, I overheard a client talking about foster children while in my store. I was interested in talking with her when I learned she was a foster parent. That is when I started to organize my thoughts around a program to provide free services to foster and homeless children. I am sure my father's friend the barber saved a lot of money giving haircuts to the eight to twelve kids he had in his house at any given time. Guess it was my turn to help out with the cost of haircuts for foster families."

Rebecca Kirtman, known as Becca by her friends, was a high school freshman at Nova High School, in Davie, Florida, when she decided she wanted to make an impact in her community and a difference in the lives of students her own age. She believed no one should miss high school events due to lack of money. As a result, Becca launched a dress drive in order to provide prom dresses and accessories free of charge. The dress drive was a success the first year, and by her sophomore year, she singlehandedly collected and donated more than two hundred and fifty formal dresses and was able to help hundreds of girls across the southern parts of Florida. Tragically, in 2003, Rebecca was killed in an automobile accident when she was only sixteen.

Wishing to keep her legacy and dream alive, friends and family members of this inspirational young lady created Becca's Closet, a nonprofit organization that not only continues to collect and donate prom dresses but also raises funds and awards post-secondary educational scholarships to young men and women who exhibit Becca's spirit and dedication to acts of generosity in their own communities. Today there are chapters of Becca's Closets in more than twenty states.

Everyone loves music of some kind, right? If you read my first book *Fostering Love: One Foster Parent's Journey*, then you know I met my wife while singing and dancing in the performing group Up With People. She was the dancer; I was the singer. Music has always been a part of my life, and it is something I treasure and try to pass along to each child that comes to my home. Whether it is introducing babies and toddlers to various genres of music, as it plays in our house all day long, having young children learn how to play piano, or the older ones take a music class in school and perhaps even join our local high school's marching band, both my wife and I feel that music can be an important healing factor for children in foster care. Music teaches so many lessons in so many different ways. We have seen many children in foster care through our home begin to thrive through music.

A few years ago, I interviewed Karyn Scott on my radio program. Karyn is the founder of Kids in a New Groove (KING), the only program in Texas to exclusively reach youth in foster care through in-home, private music lessons and mentorship. This population is notoriously underserved and frequently left out of artistic endeavors, due to the temporary nature of their ever-shifting foster care arrangements. KING removes these barriers (reliable transportation and lack of permanence), bringing the program to the student. Music mentors travel to students' homes, following students to each new placement, creating consistency in otherwise unstable lives. A student's mentor often becomes the one stable adult they can count on, with a strong bond that follows them throughout their time in foster care. As one music mentor said, "One of the most touching moments I had with my student was when his foster family invited me to his adoption at the courthouse. I'll admit, I teared up a bit seeing him get adopted into a great family with amazing parents. I'm grateful KING gave me the opportunity to meet these wonderful people and build relationships that I hope last a lifetime."

Kids in a New Groove combines the power of mentoring with music instruction, thus amplifying the relationship and providing a creative outlet for youth in foster care. Dr. James Catterall of UCLA completed a study showing "students who studied music and the arts had higher grades, scored better on standardized tests, had better attendance records and were more active in community affairs than other students." He also found that "students from poorer families who studied the arts improved overall school performance more rapidly than all other students." In both 2015, 2016, and 2017, 100 percent of eligible seniors in the KING program graduated high school, and 95 percent of those graduates pursued higher education or enlisted in the military. Through this exciting program, students develop the ability to affect positive change through the power of music and discover they can break the pattern that follows youth in foster care. Let's look at what Laura Wood, executive director of Kids in a New Groove, told me.

"Cori had endured a series of moves and shifts throughout her life. Her biological parents had given her up for adoption, and her adoptive parents, after a series of hardships, could no longer take care of her. After a few other placements, the foster care system delivered Cori to Austin, where I met her at a group home. She was fifteen years old.

"Cori loved singing when she was little. When we started lessons, she told me she hadn't been singing much lately because it reminded her of the things she was missing by moving so much—friends, teachers, family, and being a part of a school choir. After a few lessons, not only was her voice growing, her confidence was too.

"She started to realize music provided an outlet for her, a retreat, something from which she could create her own beauty no matter what surrounded her. She started to write. Her lessons shifted toward learning about text setting and chord structure and piano and arranging. She also began dressing herself colorfully, with a style that was all her own.

"When she unexpectedly lost a dear friend, she channeled that energy into music. At her request, we videoed a raw take of her covering a beautiful song she'd unearthed (she could find the coolest undiscovered stuff!), and she dedicated it to her friend and privately posted to YouTube. She said it made her feel like she had the power to do something and deal with the reality of her friend's death.

"At the KING spring recital that year, she absolutely brought the house down with her cover of 'Gold.' She styled herself for the performance, as well—I can't tell you how much she shined that day.

"Cori has since graduated from high school (where she *did* get to sing in the school choir!), a monumental feat considering everything she's been up against, and is looking forward to her future. She credits music with helping give her the confidence to be herself, to express herself, and to find herself. I credit her with reminding me how powerful it is to share music with others."

Like I said, my wife was the dancer in our group Up with People. I, on the other hand, am not a dancing machine. I wish I was. I would love to dance the night away in a respectful manner, instead of causing riots of laughter from my very two left feet. Yet, I do love dancing and have had the opportunity to watch some of my own children from foster care find joy through dancing. Like music, dance can open up many doors. The Book of Psalms tells us God loves when we dance for Him. Psalm 149:3 says, "Let them praise his name with dancing and make music to him with timbrel and harp."

As I write this, I just got off the phone with Jenna Fleetwood, who is the founder of Traveling Tutus in Florida. Having studied dance for more than twenty years, Jenna has seen firsthand how dance can change lives. She has spent her life witnessing others experience confidence, joy, and self-expression through dance. Her passion is for the broken, the hurting, and the unloved, and it has been in working with children like this that Jenna has discovered her true calling. In 2008, she graduated high school with a closet full of dance costumes she had collected from dance recitals over the years and finally needed to find a home for them before setting off for college. When she learned there wasn't an organization around that was helping repurpose used costumes, a dream was birthed in her heart. Traveling Tutus took off with unbelievable support and has since grown tremendously. Over the past eight years, Traveling Tutus has sent costumes and dance attire to hundreds of children around the world in foster care, children's homes, orphanages, and other nonprofit organizations. The outpouring of generosity from studios and dance families has been enormous. Through the giving of new and gently used dance attire, kindness and love is being shared with children around the world.

As Jenna told me, "As a foster mom myself, I can testify to the fact that I have witnessed how dance has transformed little lives. We recently took in twin three-year-old girls that had never heard of dance before. Now, after eight months of being in our care and a closet full of dance costumes, these two girls have developed into confident and joyful little princesses. It is amazing to see how a simple little dance costume can brighten a little girls' life forever!"

Now, maybe you don't give dance lessons, teach music, gather prom dresses, or even cut hair. You still have gifts, talents, and skills you can use to help children in foster care right where you live. Perhaps you could cut grass for foster parents, like a man I spoke with in Minnesota. Maybe you could build a sandbox for a foster family, like a church youth group in Texas did. In Michigan, there is a older woman who quilts blankets for all the young children entering into foster care in her home town. For those foster parents who need help transporting children, maybe you could offer to drive children to the doctor's office. Or maybe you could pay for a child in foster care to participate in a sports program or for her annual fees and dues for the school's marching band program. Whatever your talent, whatever your skill, whatever your gift, God has blessed you. How will you bless others in foster care?

QUESTIONS FOR DISCUSSION

How is the lifestyle of a foster parent different from yours?

Why might foster parents struggle and face unique stresses and challenges?

Why might visitations be difficult for a child and their family?

Where could your church or faith-based organization hold visitations or Safe Havens in your building?

How would a food ministry help a foster family?

What would it take to set up a food ministry in your church?

What kind of special gifts or talents does your church have that others in your community do not have?

Why is it important to use the gifts and talents that God has given you?

How was Cori's life changed when Kids in a New Groove helped her?

What personal gifts, talents, and skills that God blessed you with might benefit a child in foster care or a foster family in your area?

More than Just a Place to Meet

*I*n the book *Faith and Foster Care: How We Impact God's Kingdom*, I wrote about the need of foster parent support groups and associations. I have found that no one truly understands the life of a foster parent and what we experience other than another foster parent. It is a very different lifestyle, filled with unique challenges and difficulties, of heartbreaks and frustrations, and of profound joys and successes. It is important for foster parents to surround themselves with other foster parents, if only to cry with each other, share frustrations, and learn from each other. In fact, as I travel the nation, I encourage them to join a local foster parent association or support group where they can surround themselves with others who face the same experiences they face. Where there is lack of support, frustration and burn out increases, and foster parents are more likely to quit. The average length a person serves as a foster parent in the United States is a year and a half. For so many, the heartbreaks, the disappointments, and the challenges are just too much to handle.

In *Faith and Foster Care* I wrote, "A few years back, my foster parent association support group felt that we needed to move our monthly meetings to another location. We were meeting each month at our local child welfare agency. Although we appreciated the opportunity to meet there and the willingness of the agency to open their doors to us one evening each month for our training sessions and support group, it was decided that we needed to find another location, one that was more warm and inviting to the foster children in our care. After all, the local child welfare agency was a symbol to them that they were in care, and a reminder that they were not with their own families. Following some prayer about it and discussion with my fellow members of our support group and association, I placed a request in to my church and board of elders that our local association use the church's fellowship hall and kitchen facilities for our monthly meetings. The answer the church provided was one that I did not anticipate.

"It seemed that my wife and I, along with the other foster parents in our small town, had touched the hearts of many in our congregation with our act of helping our community's children. After discussion in one of the church's committees, the church granted our request to have our monthly meetings within the walls of the church my wife and I had come to love. What is even more helpful, though, is the additional help with which we have been blessed each month at the meetings. Several members of our church volunteer each month to provide our meetings with a cooked meal and child care. For my wife and me, and the other foster parents in our community, it is almost like going out on a date. Our meal is already cooked and prepared, and we have a reprieve from being foster parents, if only for a short time! For an hour or so, several adults in the church scurry the children into another part of the church with play time, arts and crafts, and various other enjoyable activities, leaving us uninterrupted while we attend a foster parenting training session, share resources and information, or just sit around a table laughing and crying together as we share stories. These meetings are ones that both my wife and I look forward to each month, and the members of the support group to which we belong are very grateful for this simple yet tremendous ministry of our church."

TAMMY'S STORY

My husband Jason and I believe God has called us to foster children in our home. Not everyone can do this—it is a joyous but heartbreaking task at times.

We have been fostering for about fourteen years, have adopted three children, and are now fostering three more. We cannot do it alone. We need prayers daily, and the children need prayers daily.

We have been so blessed over the years from churches, family, and friends. We both work out of the home, care for children, keep them in activities, and try to make them feel a part of our family. We are not rich financially but are so blessed by a smile that is priceless—not everyday, but just that one smile that says everything in that child's world is OK. So when we go on vacation or out to eat, DFCS isn't writing a check for that child to go. It is something we budget for. So when I say we appreciate all the churches have done for us—like Christmas presents for foster children, school supplies, a new pair of shoes, or simply providing a meal—we are so grateful.

The Presbyterian Church in Monticello has been a wonderful supporter of Jasper County foster parents for many years. They offer their facilities as a safe haven for family visits, keep an equipment closet, and provide meals and childcare while we have our monthly training. Our kids never want to leave and are always asking when our next meeting is. For our kids, simply making those healthy connections to a person who is interested in them and giving an hour of their time is so valuable. Most of the volunteers substitute teach or mentor at their school as well, and the kids will come home and say, "I saw that lady from the church where we go for our meetings." This church has opened its doors to us for more than ten years and supported us in so any ways—from school supplies, shoes, and Christmas presents to lots of unconditional love for us and out foster children.

DATE NIGHT

The life of a foster parent is . . . well, as you can most likely imagine, busy. Taking children to visitations with biological family members, to court, to the doctor, to school, to shop for clothes, to the therapist . . . we're always on the go. And the responsibilities continue when we are at home—helping a child sleep when he is traumatized by nightmares from his past abuse, teaching her how to write her own name when she is at least a year and a half behind academically from her peers, teaching him not to hit others, despite the fact his father heavily abused him physically, wiping away the tears because she misses her biological mother, spending hours each night getting lice out of hair. Not to mention the laundry, cooking, cleaning, housekeeping, the day job, and everything else that constitutes a normal life.

One thing my wife and I have very rarely had over the years as foster parents is a social life. No real date night. No movies together or a night out just the two of us. No shopping without children hanging on top of us. The social and romantic life of a foster parent is pretty slim, if not nonexistent.

Only recently, my wife and I were caring for eleven children in our home. Three were biological, there were adopted from foster care, and the remaining five were from foster care—a sibling group of two and another sibling group of three. Now, let me be clear. My wife and I do not have a group home, nor are we superheroes of any kind. It was simply that both sets of siblings needed to be placed that day, there was an emergency, and no other foster homes in the area were available. Thus, with some prayer and discussion, my wife and I agreed to the larger household and the impending lack of sleep sure to come our way.

Was it difficult? Absolutely! Suddenly, we had seven children in our home in diapers. That was difficult enough. There was unending laundry, cooking, cleaning, and bathing, and it was exhausting. Add to that our older children who were in the school's marching band and had homework each night. And then there were the committees and meetings my wife and I raced to and from after work, along with work, church, and so forth. Yet the addition of the various forms of traumas these children brought into our home was perhaps the most difficult part. It seemed as though each evening was spent trying to comfort a screaming child suffering from the emotional scars and traumas inflicted upon him before entering our home. My wife and I struggled with not only trying to comfort and care for these children but for all the children in our home. There was not enough time in the day to do all we needed to do. By the time we got to bed each night, we had scarcely said three words to each other all day long. We were exhausted, tired, and worn out. Not only did our own line of communication suffer as a result, but the strains and additional workload left us both too tired to spend any time with each other. As you can imagine, exhaustion led to frustration.

As I have told many foster parents over the years at training sessions and conferences, couples must focus on their own marriages from time to time while caring for children in need in their homes. Sadly, many marriages suffer during the foster process. When you put so much of your energies and time into your foster child, you may be so drained and exhausted that you soon neglect your spouse. Further complicating this, some foster children are skilled at pitting one parent against the other, bringing some heated and unproductive arguments to your home.

The idea of a date night seems pretty farfetched for most foster parents. For so many, like my wife and me, the options of respite care are few and far between. Along with that, the closest relatives my wife and I have are eighteen hours away by car, so there is little help there. Hiring a babysitter is not permitted for foster parents in many states, due to issues of state standards and regulations. Thus, as you can see, a date night for foster parents is often difficult to come by.

That's why I love the idea of what one church in Oregon is doing—the Foster Parent's Night Out (FPNO). This monthly program, held at the church, gives foster parents some hours during an evening of free respite care for all their children—whether they are adopted, biological, or foster. For many foster parents, it is an opportunity to go out to dinner, see a movie, go shopping, or even just have a few quiet hours together at home. The children at the FPNO are supervised by trained volunteers who understand the challenges children in foster care may face, why they may come into care, issues of safety, confidentiality, and strategies designed to help with behavior problems. The children enjoy fun activities and events and have the opportunity, or blessing if you will, to form another positive and healthy attachment with a loving adult—one who has their best interest in mind and the heart to help them. For children in care, the more healthy attachments and relationships they have, the better equipped they are to heal from the abuse and trauma they suffer from.

Post-Adoption Support

I never set out to be an adoptive parent.

There, I said it.

After the loss of our first child from anencephaly, a condition where the brain fails to develop, we were blessed with three healthy children over the next six years. Then we became foster parents, as we wanted to help children who were suffering. When one of our children from foster care came up for adoption, I did not initially wish to adopt her. You see, I felt that if I adopted her, I would be taking her away from a family who could not have children. In my mind at the time, God blessed me with three children of my own, and adopting this new one would be a selfish act on my behalf. Fortunately, my wife, our church, our friends and family, and the Good Lord convinced me that child who had been living in my home for twenty-two months, since she was five days old, was truly my own, and she was a gift of God to my family. Through the years, my family has been blessed with the adoption of two more children, and I could not be more delighted. There truly is no difference between my biological and adopted children.

Journalists often ask me how the adoption process works in the foster care system. Let's examine what I wrote in the article, "A Forever Family: Adoption from Foster Care" for *Medium*.[8] "When a child is placed into foster care, the initial goal is to have the child reunified with his birth parents or a member of his biological family. To be sure, the initial intent of placing a child into care is that the placement be temporary, with reunification the main objective. Yet, there are those instances when reunification is not possible, and the child is placed through the court system for adoption.

"Of the over 560,000 children placed in foster care in 2010, it is estimated that 107,000 of these foster children became eligible for adoption. Sadly, only around 53,000 of these children were adopted during that year, with over half of these children being adopted by foster parents, with the rest being adopted by family members, and a small percentage being adopted by non-relatives (AFCARS 2012). . . . For those children who are not adopted, many remain in the foster care system for extended periods of time. Some of these children are moved to group homes, while others simply age out of the foster care system, never truly finding a family of their own and a place to call home.

"There are several reasons why a foster child might be placed up for adoption. First, the custody rights of the birth parents are voluntarily terminated; second, the custody rights of the birth parents are terminated by a court order; and third, the child is up for adoption due to the death of birth parents.

"As foster parents, there are many reasons why we are the ideal choice to adopt a foster child. Many times when a child from foster care has his rights terminated, he has already been living in a loving and stable home with his foster family. When we care for foster children, we raise them as our own for an extended amount of time, meeting his needs, and nurturing him since he was removed from his birth parent's home. . . . [These foster parents are] the ones most familiar with these needs, and have gained valuable insight and resources to best . . . care for the foster child." Scripture speaks often on adoption.

> HE DEFENDS THE CAUSE OF THE FATHERLESS AND THE WIDOW,
> AND LOVES THE FOREIGNER RESIDING AMONG YOU,
> GIVING THEM FOOD AND CLOTHING.
> —DEUTERONOMY 10:18

> DEFEND THE WEAK AND THE FATHERLESS;
> UPHOLD THE CAUSE OF THE POOR AND THE OPPRESSED.
> —PSALM 82:3

> GOD DECIDED IN ADVANCE TO ADOPT US INTO HIS OWN FAMILY BY
> BRINGING US TO HIMSELF THROUGH JESUS CHRIST. THIS IS WHAT
> HE WANTED TO DO, AND IT GAVE HIM GREAT PLEASURE.
> —EPHESIANS 1:5 NLT

> TO LOOK AFTER ORPHANS AND WIDOWS IN THEIR DISTRESS
> AND TO KEEP ONESELF FROM BEING POLLUTED BY THE WORLD.
> —JAMES 1:27

As exciting, joyous, and wonderful as adoption can be, there are often challenges afterwards, challenges much of society often does not see nor understand. After an adoption has been finalized, the children may have a difficult time accepting the fact that they will never return to live with their biological parents or birth family members again. Children who have been adopted from foster care often need time to grieve the loss of connection with their birth family. He may very well need time to experience the stages of grief before he fully transfers attachment from his birth family to his new forever family. Even though he may have lived with the foster family for a long period of time, he will likely reexperience feelings of loss during the adoption process. After all, his birth family gave him his appearance and gender, his intelligence, his temperament, talents, and of course, his life.

You no doubt realize by now that most children who are placed in foster care have suffered some type of emotional, physical, and/or sexual abuse, as well as other trauma in their lives. Add to the daily anxieties they face as they struggle with these forms of abuse, it should come as no surprise that even after an adoption has been finalized, the anxieties and traumas will continue. Brain development and developmental delays in language, learning, and behavior are also often lifelong challenges from their exposure to traumatic experiences and abuse, even after adoption. Finally, post-adoption challenges may also include issues of trust and attachment for the child and his new forever family.

What you may not realize, though, is that many adoptive parents experience depression post-adoption. It is estimated that between 18–26 percent of adoptive mothers suffer from what is known as Post Adoption Depression. As these new adoptive parents struggle not only with their own feelings, they also face the emotional post adoption challenges their children face. Quite often, adoptive parents suffering from Post Adoption Depression are overwhelmed and do not know where or to whom to turn.

Is the church helping post-adoptive families who have adopted children from foster care? Sadly, when I posed this same question to foster parents who have adopted, I was deeply troubled by the responses I received.

PERSONAL STORIES

———o———

Our churches have not done anything special. We even had a church that baptizes infants regularly refuse to baptize my adopted child because he was too old at eighteen months. —Anonymous

Our adopted daughter has a developmental delay and severe anxiety (undiagnosed at the time, but this momma knew something was wrong and what she needed, even without a name). The church nursery coordinator was a harsh disciplinarian and rule follower who would not allow my girl to remain in a younger classroom. My daughter was terrified of her teacher's abrasive manner. She was so hung up on the rules of ages in classes that my daughter suffered. It was easier on my family to just stop going than to fight yet another battle on Sunday and Wednesday nights. I so desperately wish someone would have understood how much it took just to get us through those doors. To be discouraged once inside was more than we could deal with after a while, so we just quit going. I know there are churches that nurture and love like crazy, and we had really good people in place who loved us, but those people weren't running the nursery or making the rules. *One* unbendable woman—that is all it took to break our spirits. Normally, a person like her wouldn't get to me, but when you are exhausted from raising a post-trauma kid and searching for answers and struggling just to show up, *one* person can break you. —Anonymous

LESLIE'S STORY

———o———

We adopted four times. The first time we adopted a five-year-old girl with cleft from China. The church did help us a little financially with the adoption, but after the church "split," that was it. There was no follow-up from a member, no meeting in the airport, no visits, no phone calls, and no meals. The church is still in operation, and the same members are there. Actually we *just* moved membership in the last year. We've added three more children to your family in that time and still nothing. My mom goes to church there, so they are aware.

Our second adoption was a severely disabled child from China. We were at a different church. This time we received no money, and again no help. During this same time we found out I had cancer and our newly adopted son was dying from a neurological disease. Again, no call. No meal. Nothing. I was told we weren't members so they wouldn't help us.

The next two adoptions were from foster care. We started in a big mega church, and honestly not that many people knew us there, so again we received no support. When we finalized the adoption, we are at a smaller church, where we still attend, so everyone knows our situation. Our daughter has surgeries, our son is sick and unable to do much, our girls adopted from foster care have fetal alcohol syndrom, and my husband works three jobs. They know. But no one reaches out. We haven't been to church in a few weeks. No one calls. I have said "we are struggling," but no one reaches out.

CASSANDRA'S STORY

We adopted two children from foster care while at two different churches. Neither church helped or did anything to support our adoption afterwards. We were even foster parents for four years. At the second church, we were in a leadership role and had been having severe struggles with our middle child, our daughter. She came to us at age two. We tried everything—therapy, medication, family therapy. She received in-patient treatment multiple times. Things just got worse and worse. We sought help from the church but received nothing. Then came the false allegations. Thankfully, nothing came of those, but her aggression got worse and worse and resulted in lies that were out of this world and even destruction of property. We didn't know what to do. Her last two in-patient hospitalizations both recommended a long-term residential stay. We were exhausted. Still we received no help or support from the church. She went to a psychiatric residential treatment facility for a year. And though she was still extremely aggressive and violent, insurance said they weren't going to pay any longer. We felt we were unable to bring her home and filed a petition for a private child in need of care hoping that would get the state's attention and get us more help. Nope. Unfortunately, we ended up relinquishing our rights. Our pastoral team knew exactly what was going on but provided no support. When we explained our situation to the leadership team and told them we were leaving the team for a time to rest and renew, we heard from not a single person who attended that meeting to see how we were doing. That meeting happened three-and-a-half years ago. And we have not been back to a church since.

Now, I share those stories with you not to drag you down or depress you but because I feel it is important for all of us to realize that for some foster and adoptive parents, the church as a whole is failing them. This breaks my heart, and I imagine it does the same for you, as well. Let's make sure we change that perception.

Like foster parent support groups, adoptive parents need support through community, as well. This is yet another area that those of faith can help spread the power of God's love. Churches and faith-based groups can open their assembly halls, their Sunday school rooms, their kitchens, and their doors and host monthly adoption support groups. As an adoptive parent myself, I can assure you these support groups are important, just like the support groups for foster parents.

Adoption support groups offer so much for those who have had the blessing of bringing another child into their home through adoption. Like the foster parent support groups, adoption support groups allow adoptive parents to surround themselves with a community of people who have similar experiences, challenges, and struggles. These support groups allow adoptive parents to validate their own feelings and frustrations with others who have experienced these same frustrations and feelings. Along with that, adoptive parents can also celebrate the many successes and joys unique to adoptive families. When adoptive parents come together, they are able to share resources, offer suggestions to problems others may be facing, and be of support to them during challenging times. It's a wonderful opportunity for adoptive parents to come together and lift up each other and the children in prayer.

That empty room not being used on Tuesday nights, the large congregational hall sitting unused on Saturday afternoons, the volunteers looking for ways to be involved, all can be used to support foster and adoptive parents. Whether it is by providing meeting space for support groups or hosting date nights for foster or adoptive parents, your church may just be the perfect space and setting of support.

QUESTIONS FOR DISCUSSION

What is the church in Monticello, Georgia, doing that is so helpful to Tammy and her fellow foster families?

Why is it important for people of faith to help foster families in their area?

What would a foster parent support group look like in your own church?

Why is a date night important for foster parents? Why is it important for married foster parents to have time alone together?

This chapter had several examples from foster parents concerning how churches and people of faith have hurt them in some way. How have you seen people of faith hurt others?

Who are the "weak and fatherless" where you live, as described in Psalm 82:3?

Can you share a story of a family you know that has adopted a child?

Why does God want His people to adopt and look after children in need?

Why would a church or place of faith be a good location to host a foster parent or adoption support group meeting?

How would a support group for foster families or adoptive families be a form of ministry?

CLOTHING THE LEAST OF THESE

The call came at 6:30 that night while we sat around the table eating dinner. As is often the case, the child needed placement immediately, and the caseworker needed an answer from us. We had been foster parents for five years at that point, and my wife and I had the agreement we would only care for children who were no older than our own children, as we were concerned about exposing our children to lifestyles they were not ready for yet. This time, though, we had a decision to make.

"John, we have an emergency where we need to place a child for a few days until his uncle comes up from Florida to get him," Cathy, the caseworker, told me over the phone.

As a foster parent I had to quickly determine if my home was the best environment for him, and if it was a good fit for my family. With that in mind, I had a number of questions to ask, all designed to help Kelly and I make the decision if we could help care for this child or not. "How old is he?" I asked the caseworker.

"He's thirteen, and he was found living under a highway overpass this morning a half hour away from y'all," the caseworker replied. I could hear the anxiousness in her own voice, as she was desperately trying to find a family who would help this child and take him into their home.

Thirteen? Sensing my reluctance from the silence on my end of the line, Cathy added, "I know y'all don't want any older children, and I understand if y'all say no. I just had to call and ask."

"Cathy," I said with uncertainty, "can I talk with Kelly and pray about it and then call you back?"

"Absolutely, John. Thanks."

"No problem. Thank you, Cathy; I'll call you back in a few minutes. Talk to you then." As I hung up the phone, I put my head down on the counter for a second, trying to digest what just happened.

"Well?" Kelly sat at the table, waiting for me to recover. I quickly repeated what Cathy had to say, and looked to her for an opinion. She frowned. "A thirteen-year-old boy could pose some real problems for our children. We don't know what he's been through or what he might say. I'm worried he might do something. I don't know, John; what do you think?"

"I agree; you're right. We don't know what he'll do or say. That's a tough age. But, it's just for a few days, like Cathy said. What do you want to do?" I asked. I wasn't real sure, myself, on how I felt about it. This was a different situation, a tough decision. How would this boy affect our own children?

"I don't know," she paused, before adding, "let's pray." Holding the phone in one hand, I walked over to her, taking her hand in my free one. Once again, we looked to God for guidance.

After finishing our prayer, I asked, "Well, shall I call Cathy back and tell her . . . what?"

"Tell her we can do it," Kelly answered, with a forced smile.

Later that evening, thirteen-year-old C. J. arrived at our home. Like so many children before him, our newest child from foster care arrived with only the clothes on his back. Nothing else. No jacket, no toothbrush, no comb, no book bag, no pajamas. Nothing at all.

It was C. J.'s birthday. Earlier in the day, his mother had been driving him on a busy highway in a large city near our home. Pulling over to the side of the road underneath a highway overpass, C. J.'s mother asked her only son to get out of the car and get his presents out of the trunk. When he did as his mother had asked, closing the front passenger door, where he had been seated, his mother then drove off. That's right! The mother deserted her thirteen-year-old son on the highway—on his birthday.

Later, at 2:00 a.m., as the thirteen-year-old was trying his best not to let Kelly or me hear him crying as he tried to silence his sobs in his pillow, I got out of bed and quickly got dressed. Driving to a nearby twenty-four-hour chain store, I not only bought the teenager some clothing, school supplies, and toiletries, I also bought him a skateboard, a basketball, and some other birthday presents. The next morning, as we threw a birthday celebration for our newest family member, it was the clothing he was most grateful for.

For many foster children, this case is all too real, and is a sad reality for both foster parents and foster children. With the many cuts in budget for child welfare agencies across the United States, foster parents are receiving fewer funds from these agencies, making it more difficult to provide for the foster children that come in and out of their homes. To make matters worse, the poor economy has also left many foster parents with less money as they strive to provide such basic necessities as clothing for growing children. As a result, foster parents across the country are struggling to provide for the children under their care.[9]

Over and over again, our Heavenly Father reminds us we are to clothe His children. Scripture is abundant in this manner.

> IS IT NOT TO DIVIDE YOUR BREAD WITH THE HUNGRY
> AND BRING THE HOMELESS POOR INTO THE HOUSE;
> WHEN YOU SEE THE NAKED, TO COVER HIM;
> AND NOT TO HIDE YOURSELF FROM YOUR OWN FLESH?
> —ISAIAH 58:7 NASB

> AND HE WOULD ANSWER AND SAY TO THEM, "THE MAN
> WHO HAS TWO TUNICS IS TO SHARE WITH HIM WHO HAS NONE;
> AND HE WHO HAS FOOD IS TO DO LIKEWISE."
> —LUKE 3:11 NASB

> I NEEDED CLOTHES AND YOU CLOTHED ME, I WAS SICK AND YOU
> LOOKED AFTER ME, I WAS IN PRISON AND YOU CAME TO VISIT ME.
> —MATTHEW 25:36

> BUT [HE] GIVES HIS FOOD TO THE HUNGRY
> AND PROVIDES CLOTHING FOR THE NAKED.
> —EZEKIEL 18:16

Many churches and nonprofit faith-based organizations have created what are commonly referred to as clothes closets. When a child comes into care in a community, churches and faith-based groups across the nation spring forth to work alongside the town's foster parent association and make sure each child has clothes.

Clothes closets offer for free, gently used or new clothing and apparel for children in foster care. Some clothes closets are set up like a business or clothing store, equipped with fitting rooms, and may even wrap or box items, just like a true clothing store. I have been in some foster care clothes closets that offer more than clothing, such as jewelry, purses, toiletries, toys, school supplies, or other items a child might wish for or need.

Foster care closets are not only helpful for the child, as it allows them to "shop" for their own clothing in a professional like setting, but it is also of great benefit to the foster parent who has received a child unexpectedly or late at night and does not have time to go from one store to another, gathering clothes for a child who has none. All clothing and other items in these clothes closet are donated. Even those who are unable to donate materials can donate of their time as volunteers to staff the facilities.

Tammy McGuire saw the plight of foster children coming into her own home in the state of Florida. When two foster boys were placed into her home with trash bags full of clothing that was simply unwearable, she decided to make a change in her own community. So Tammy began the Foster Closet. Starting in a closet in her home with bins of clothes and other items for her own foster children, as well as for others in her community, she knew she needed to do more. First she borrowed two rooms in her town's child welfare agency and then moved into a storage unit after outgrowing the agency's space. Today, the Foster Closet is run from a 5,000-square-foot freestanding building centrally located for her five-county area. Using James 1:27, which commands us "to look after orphans [or fatherless]" as their source for inspiration, their motto is, "Our children have stains on the inside and don't need to wear them on the out." Since 2009, the Foster Closet seeks to provide not just stuff but also treasured memories with a doll, a car, or an action hero.

"I truly believe that if we are willing to look for His purpose," Tammy says, "He will direct us to the true meaning of "His kingdom on earth." God wants us to be ever changing and growing through education of our foster care system. I challenge each person to be His vessel and to shine His light into our world of fostering."

Foster Closet allows children and caregivers to "shop" for free in the store. The Foster Closet Corp provides each child with at least seven outfits, two pairs of shoes, a winter coat, summer bathing suit, new socks and undergarments, two pajamas, hygiene products, ten books, and even purses, jewelry, maternity, and prom dresses for those foster girls who are of age. They also provide high chairs, beds, bikes, video games, and Bibles. Since Foster Closet became a 501c3 in 2009, they have help more than eight hundred children a year.

The Foster Closet also offers a program called Pathway, which provides additional help to those foster children who turn eighteen and qualify for the Independent Living Program with beds, sofas, televisions, dressers, kitchen and bathroom items, and anything else a young adult might need in their new home. Pathway delivers the items to the new apartment and their donors and volunteers transform the shell of an apartment into a home.[10]

Foster Closet has a monthly support group where they offer foster parents and their children dinner, childcare, and a group session lead by a licensed clinical social worker. The foster parents are given a safe place to find guidance and support.

Recently, Tammy became an advocate for a national organization called The Forgotten Initiative. Tammy has partnered the Foster Closet with TFI to begin a parent's night out for foster, relative, and nonrelative caregivers. Caregivers can drop off their children for two hours at a local church, where workers from another nonprofit, Kim's Open Door, provide dinner and lead the children in a fun, biblically based curriculum.

As the Foster Closet is a nonprofit organization, it relies upon donations and volunteers and hosts two to three fundraisers per year. Foster Closet also receives funding from a local community-based care agency. In addition to the volunteers needed to run their programs and answer the phone, Foster Closet depends on twenty-five to thirty-five volunteers to help run the store. They also works with local high school clubs, corporate businesses, and local churches.

There are hundreds of such foster care closets across the nation, many located in churches and faith-based nonprofit organizations. Through clothes drives, contributions, and donations, both children and foster parents are being blessed by this incredible clothes ministry.

THE FEELING OF BEING GARBAGE, THE GIFT OF DIGNITY

Imagine moving countless times from one home to another, from one family to another family. Known as multiple displacement, the act of moving from home to home in foster care is not unfamiliar for a child.

Perhaps a foster family is unable to give the care a child deserves. Or maybe the child's parents have moved, and the child needs to be moved as well to remain close to the birth family. Or the child may be able to return home to their birth family then, due to circumstances, be placed back into foster care and into yet another home. The child may run away from their foster home only to be caught and placed into another home, group home, or even a juvenile center. There are many reasons a foster child may move several times. I have worked with some children who have been in up to thirty different homes throughout their young lives. You can imagine what that does to a child's sense of worth, their sense of trust, and their feelings of attachment.

And yet what compounds multiple displacement is how they move. Yes, *how* they move. Far too many children in foster care arrive at their new foster home with their few belongings shoved quickly into a black trash bag. A trash bag half full with a few changes of clothing, a toy, maybe a picture. Slung over their shoulder, they uncomfortably carry their few possessions and belongings from one home to another. It is humiliating, it is embarrassing, and it is yet another reminder that they are a child in foster care.

Let's be clear. Every child deserves to be treated better than trash. Every child deserves to feel more valued than garbage. Every child deserves to have some sense of dignity.

Many churches and nonprofit associations across the nation have responded to the call for caring for children in foster care by launching suitcase drives and collecting bags for children in care. These groups see the need and are determined to bring a sense of dignity to a child by giving the child a sense of self-worth as he or she leaves one home and moves to another, whether temporarily or permanently. Along with suitcases, many organizations collect duffel bags and backpacks. For some organizations, the suitcase, duffel bag, or school bag might be all they supply. For other organizations, these suitcases and bags are filled with a variety of things, including blankets, pajamas, a few comfortable changes of clothing, a coat or jacket, undergarments, socks, and even toiletries.

Linda Coolbaugh is the founder of a small organization in Wyoming that is making a big difference to children in foster care. Out of her own home, Linda runs Suitcases Make Individuals' Lives Easier, otherwise known as SMILE. SMILE provides various small necessities to children who find themselves suddenly placed in foster care and is run by just one person, Linda. Perhaps we should let Linda explain in her own words.

Linda's Story

I have belonged to the Bowman's Creek Free Methodist Church now for many years. That is where I heard the story of one of our pastor's children they fostered and adopted. It was sad to hear how, while going through these changes of residence, they are handed a bag and told to fill it. I already knew from experience that these children are starting all over, some with nothing at all. Our pastor discussed a project to collect book bags and fill them with some essential needs.

Children are often placed in foster care in emergency situations. It's 2 a.m. and suddenly they're removed from their homes. They're told to take what they need and toss it into a bag. Children who find themselves in such circumstances are often short of such necessities as a toothbrush, comb, or shampoo.

I don't work directly with any of the children but have been thanked many times by those who work with the children, letting me know how much it's needed and that I have helped many. They tell me how much the foster parents tell them to thank me. I know this was my calling from God, and I hope to continue as long as possible.

Recently, I met a group at a church that went even further in this form of ministry. As their hearts were touched by the stories that many of these children placed into foster care never had a word of comfort or a gesture of kindness, they decided to fill duffel bags for each child that came into foster care in their community. Some of these colorful duffel bags were filled not only with clothing, but also a small stuffed animal, a football or basketball, or a truck or doll. Each had a nightlight, a journal, a children's Bible, and a handwritten note of support. Members of the church prayed over each bag and asked for God's blessings upon the child who might receive it.

Whether your church or faith-based group donates the suitcases and bags of love to the children themselves or to a local foster care agency or foster parent association, please know one thing. Although you may never see the suitcase in the hands of a child, know that somewhere a child is holding his brand new suitcase that he can call his own, is feeling a little better, and is finding comfort in the knowledge that someone cares about him.

Back To School

When I first began teaching, and before I was a foster parent, I knew very little about foster care or about foster children. To be sure, what I thought I knew about children in foster care, and about the foster care system, was as far from the truth as possible. Like most of the general public, I had false ideas and beliefs about foster children, and much of it was negative, I am afraid to say. This was due mainly to the false stereotypes that abound in society. As a result, I was not prepared to meet the many needs that the students from foster homes so desperately needed while in my classroom. Even further, in all my years of college, and of additional instructional workshops, I did not have the training required to best help foster children as they struggled in my classroom, and neither did my colleagues.

After a few foster children had passed through my own home, I began to appreciate the fact that I had to not only adjust my teaching habits for foster children, but I also had to become my own foster children's advocate at their own schools. I watched my foster children struggle in my fellow teacher's classrooms, and also was witness to these same teachers as they failed to understand the various emotional challenges the children in my home were going through on a daily basis. To be sure, there were those times when I had to politely intervene on behalf of my foster child. There were also those times when I had to sit across the table from a fellow teacher as we discussed how my foster child's behavior was interfering in the classroom setting. My desire to better assist both my colleagues and foster children led to my doctoral studies on the subject. I simply wanted to help children in foster care succeed in school, as well as bring awareness about their struggles to our schools.

Foster children, in general, tend to perform below level in regard to both academic performance and in positive behavior than those students who come from either traditional homes as well as children from economically disadvantaged homes. The majority of children under foster care supervision experience problems in behavior while enrolled in public schools. Those foster children who were taken from homes due to neglect repeatedly suffer from a number of developmental delays. These include poor language and vocabulary development, thus impairing communication skills.

For many children in foster care, our schools are the last place they want to be. For that foster child who has been taken from his family, from his home, from his friends, and all he knows, and suddenly placed into a strange home late one evening only to be forced to attend a strange school the following day, it is incredibly traumatic. Foster children often have a difficult time with exhibiting proper school behavior during the school day. For many of the children, school is a constant reminder that they are, indeed, foster children without a true home. The continuous reminder that their peers are living with biological family members while they are not is a difficult reality for them and can be manifested in several ways. Some foster children simply withdraw and become antisocial in an attempt to escape their current environment and world they have been thrust into. For many foster children, violent behavior becomes the norm, as they not only act out in a negative and disruptive fashion in the school, but in their foster home too, prompting yet another move to another foster home and another school.[11]

Make no mistake; sometimes the difference between a positive school experience and a negative one is the little details that are often overlooked. It is so important to not only help children in foster care in school throughout the year, but also help them get off to a great start to begin with—whether with tutoring or by providing school supplies, something foster children often do not have.

Churches and faith-based groups often host back-to-school drives for youth in their community who are in foster care. Many organizations, Sunday school classes, and church volunteers stuff school backpacks with paper, pencils, pens, folders, notebooks, crayons, markers, highlighters, glue sticks, calculators, erasers, scissors, rulers, tissue, wipes, hand sanitizers, and even combs, brushes, and deodorants. As a foster parent myself, I can assure you that not only are you helping the children in your area, you are also helping the foster parents in a tremendous way. For many foster parents, the cost of school supplies only adds to the financial stresses and challenges of caring for children in need. When your church helps with donating school supplies to the foster children in your area, you are helping to not only ease the financial needs of foster parents but also freeing them of the time to shop for these supplies as well, time a foster parent often does not have.

DEBBY'S STORY

Most of us can only imagine what a child or youth feels being removed from their caregiver, home, community, school, etc. with very possessions. No warm jacket, favorite toy, blanket, book bag, mommy, daddy, nothing from their world. An excellent picture of this is the children's book *A Different Home*. This was my go-to book as an elementary school teacher to help a child work through this process. It may seem to us that their new situation is much improved by being removed from their home, but in their heart, a new place is not home. *A Different Home* verbalizes just this on the child's level and opens doors for discussion.

After sharing this book one particular time with a new foster child in my classroom, the student asked if he could take it home to read to his siblings, who were all placed into the same foster care home with him. This student kept the book in his book bag, and I truly believe it helped him realize it was going to be okay.

He even asked me if he could read it to the class one day. As he read the book, my face was filled with tears. He did a beautiful job. He announced to the class, "I'm a foster child," and it brought us all closer together as a school family.

The Mercy, Love and Joy mission is a program of a church I attend in middle Georgia. One of their ministries is to provide school supplies for children in our area each school year. Foster children are a main emphasis, all through the year, and we are available to do anything we can for them at any time. This includes book bags available and packed with supplies as soon as they arrive at our school door, as well as shoes, clothes, jackets, glasses, toiletries, and any specials needs. It is often as healing for those helping as for the children or youth being helped. Is it not what we can do to shows Gods love?

Questions for Discussion

Why did C. J. not have any clothes or belongings to call his own?

How might it feel for you if your own child, grandchild, or special child in your life was forced to move to a foster home and had no clothing of their own? How might they feel?

Why do most children in foster care not have any belongings when they arrive at a new foster home?

How is the Foster Closet helping foster parents in Florida?

How big is the homeless situation for children where you live?

What do the words in Matthew 25:36 mean to you? How does this verse call people of faith to action?

How can a simple act of donating a new suitcase to a child in foster care help restore a child's dignity?

How can your church of faith-based organization help children in foster care with school supplies?

CELEBRATING THE CHILD

"Happy Birthday!" are two words every child deserves to have said and sung to them each year. Every child deserves to have a birthday party thrown in their honor. I am sure you had a few birthday parties thrown for you when you were a child. You may have even thrown a few for a child of your own. They are special times and special days for a child, creating memories that can last a lifetime—birthday cakes, ice cream, balloons, wrapped presents, and friends and family members surrounding the birthday child, all making a big fuss, and a big to-do for a child on his special day.

Sadly, for far too many children in foster care, a birthday is something that is never celebrated in his honor. Even sadder, the words, "Happy Birthday," are never said to him, never sung to him. I have witnessed this time again in our own home.

As I write this, several come to mind, but one in particular stands out. Scotty was seven years old and had been living with us for three months by the time his birthday rolled around. Scotty had suffered great neglect, as well as physical abuse. Scotty's mother was a drug addict and had been living with several boyfriends though the years who in turn abused Scotty physically. Scotty's mother did nothing to interfere on behalf of her son, did nothing to protect the child who called her "Mommy." Scotty had never known his father. When Scotty arrived at our home one winter evening, he was scared, confused, anxious, and suffering from severe malnutrition. The first several months with him were rocky as Scotty often lashed out at my wife and me with anger and resentment in an attempt to process feelings.

In mid spring, Scotty's eighth birthday came around, and we were determined to make is a special day for our son from foster care. In our home, my wife loves to celebrate a birthday in a large way. We begin on the morning of the birthday by waking the birthday person with breakfast in bed, as all in the house sing, "Happy Birthday." The birthday person gets to choose their favorite cereal (a big treat when my wife is a doctor of nutrition, as many of these cereals don't pass her judgment during the year!) and a glass of fresh juice. A few presents are opened, with the rest saved for after school, along with birthday cake, homemade ice cream, songs, and laughter.

On this particular birthday morning, as we sang "Happy Birthday" to Scotty, we were sadly not surprised when the now eight-year-old did not know the words to this timeless and age-old song. Tragically, we had seen this happen with several other children who had come to live with us over the years. No one had ever sung "Happy Birthday" to them before. What touched my heart, though, that morning was when Scotty opened his birthday present.

Wrapped in colorful red wrapping paper, tenderly and lovingly done by my wife the night before, Scotty was unsure how to open the first present given to him. At eight years old, no one had ever given him a wrapped present before. After encouraging cheers from my wife and me, along with our children, Scotty very carefully began to peel off the tape, taking great care not to rip the wrapping paper. My son was not going to have any of that, though, telling his foster brother to "Rip it open!" As paper flew, Scotty's smile began to spread. The child who had never known kindness earlier in his life, and had only known verbal, emotional, and physical abuse, had opened his very first birthday present. By opening this wrapped gift, hope was also opened, the hope that just maybe, his life would get a little better.

Perhaps this child's birthday party was a small event, but for Scotty, it is so much more. This very simple gesture can be a wonderful chance to heal from the trauma and lack of love in a child's life. Wouldn't you agree that every child deserves to have "Happy

Birthday" sung to him? Every child deserves the chance to blow out candles on his day. After all, a child's birthday should be a day of joy, hope, love, and celebration. Sadly for so many children, it is a day that is ignored, a day that is forgotten, and is a day that brings sadness and pain.

CHRISTY'S STORY

Our former foster child is one of three siblings; two siblings went to one foster home, and the other child went to ours. We were heartbroken for the separation from each other, and as the parental rights were terminated, we worried they would not be adopted together. Our family unfortunately was not a good fit for all three, but we saw they should stay together if they could. Over time, we were filled with heartache for our foster son's siblings as we learned what they had experienced and what they continued to experience in their time in foster care. We prayed all along for them, but my desire was for something more proactive, something to make them feel special and help them escape the difficulties they faced, even if just for a short time. Finally, the idea came to me. What if we had a special tea party, a special memory just for these kids? We wouldn't have it on a holiday or birthday, which would be more of a set-up for emotions running high. We wouldn't invite other kids, even our own biological kids (though we made sure they did a little something special at the same time). We would set it up just for these three children.

But I couldn't do it alone. My husband and I have no family in the city where we live. With location options already booked or too expensive, our church offered a space for free. My friend from church baked special cookies, helped us decorate, and helped with all the little details so I could focus on the kids. Other friends came and took pictures, provided a tea set and decorations, and dressed as favorite characters to be invited to the special tea party. Family members of mine that couldn't be there donated to cover the cost of costumes, decorations, and a photo book keepsake.

The kids were in awe when the characters came and greeted them, and they got to sit at a very fancy table. The oldest child asked question after question while the younger two smiled shyly and quietly as they ate cookies and drank hot cocoa. They decorated crowns together, and the kids put stickers in the helpers' hair, and giggled and giggled and giggled. Later, they went upstairs to have a singalong to some favorite Disney songs with the characters. They danced around in a circle with the characters, all singing joyfully and with such freedom that my foster mom friend and I couldn't help but tear up a little. It ended at just the right time for the kids, and as we buckled into the van, one little one said with wide eyes, "That party was awesome."

I hope others will read this and think of something that would be just right for a sibling group or a child in foster care that's having a hard time—something they will love and not be overwhelmed by. Something that shows tenderness and says, "You are special."

The great ending to this story is that the siblings *are* being adopted together by a wonderful family. We are very happy to still be in touch, and while we planned this party worrying about the worst-case scenario, that it could one of their few or last memories together, we know now it was a happy memory among many happy memories to come.

Like Christy, many churches and faith-based organizations are helping to make that special day for children in foster care just that: special. A day set aside just for them. A day dedicated to celebrating who they are. A birthday. People of Christ are planning birthday parties for kids in foster care in their own churches, complete with streamers, party hats, balloons, cake, ice cream, and a load of presents. By working with their local foster care agency or foster parent association, these faith-based groups are planning with those who care for children in foster care on how to best celebrate that child. Whether it is by offering space in their church for foster parents to have a special birthday party, or hosting the party themselves, churches are finding this to be a joy-filled form of outreach.

Other groups donate birthday decorations, food, candles, balloons, and wrapped toys and gifts to foster parents in their area or to foster parent agencies. Churches host toy drives. One faithful member, who was celebrating ninety years of age, asked her family members to spend that money they would have spent on her party and gifts on a child in foster care in the small town she lived in. (Remember, she was ninety! There was reason to celebrate!)

Every child deserves a birthday cake. Every child deserves to have a present with his name on it. Every child deserves to have hope.

Making It a Merry Christmas

You know the familiar phrase, "'Tis the season to be jolly." Well Christmas is not a jolly season for the roughly half a million children in foster care in the United States. It is often a time of great sadness and despair, a time of loneliness and of rejection. For these children, it is a reminder of the anxiety and trauma in their young lives. Many foster children are faced with the realization that they will not be "home for the holidays" with their biological family members. It is a reminder that they are separated from their parents and family.

I have a question for you. Do you remember waking up as a child on Christmas morning? If you were like me, you couldn't wait to get your parents up and dash into the room where your Christmas tree was. Wrapping paper flew, screams of joy and surprise filled the air, and great food and family surrounded you; it was truly a magical day. I imagine you have fond memories of it. I also imagine you probably carry on some of the traditions you grew up with and share them with your own children or even your grandchildren. For most of us, Christmas is a time of family, a time of joy, and a reminder of God's love for each of us. It is also a time where we hope and pray for peace on earth, good will to all men.

When children in foster care wake up Christmas morning, they are surrounded by people who just may be strangers to them. It is a stark reminder to these children that they are not with their own family. Families are supposed to be together during the holidays, yet these children in care are not. They may not know when they will see them next.

More than likely, a foster child will have feelings of sadness and grief as he is separated from his own family during this time of celebration. After all, this separation is during a time that is supposed to be centered *on* the family. Quite simply, they want to go home and live with their family members, despite the abuse and trauma they may have suffered from them and despite all you can and do offer and provide.

The church can help during such a time. Each December, I read story after story of churches and faith-based organizations helping children in foster care during Christmastime by offering toy drives, gift wrapping, and donations to foster care agencies, among other acts.

Once, as I was walking off the stage from speaking at a foster parent conference, a foster mother approached me. It was apparent she was eager to speak to me. As I listened, she told me how one church in her town was helping foster children. For several years, the church had opened their doors and hosted a Christmas party for all the foster children in that town. Not only were the children invited, but they also invited the foster parents and the birth parents. All were invited to come, as the church saw it as an opportunity to witness God's love.

The Christmas party is truly a large celebration! Church volunteers help the children, as well as the adults, make their own handcrafted ornaments they can take home and have throughout their lives. Both foster parents and biological family members are able to sit down at a table and create personal Christmas ornaments. Another table is set up for creating gingerbread houses and decorating Christmas cookies. Youth can get temporary Christmas tattoos and play Christmas games. At the end of the party, Santa Claus and Mrs. Claus make an appearance. Santa always has a bag full of wrapped gifts for the children. Each child gets several gifts, all wrapped and with their names on each gift. After Santa hands out the gifts, the children and adults have the opportunity to have their picture taken with Santa and Mrs. Claus. (I have several pictures of myself on Santa's lap—to both the joy and chagrin of my children!) These Christmas parties are not only special for the children, but they are special for the biological family members as well. As they watch their children healing through laughter, filled with love, and experiencing joy by those who care for them, a part of that biological family member and birth parent begins to heal from their own personal trauma. Truly, a Christmas miracle for all!

Just like with birthdays, faith-based organizations are reaching out to children in foster care and helping during this season of His birth. There are a number of ways faith-based groups can help with those in foster care. Whether it is sponsoring a child and providing him with presents, gifts, and clothing; throwing a Christmas party; hosting a toy drive or Christmas party; donating a Christmas tree to a foster family in your area; baking Christmas cookies alongside the children; or even inviting a foster family in your area to go Christmas caroling with your church, faith-based groups can not only help children in care but foster and birth parents as well.

Special organizations also play a role in ministering to foster families. Let's look at what Holly is doing in the state of Georgia.

HOLLY'S STORY

I started and run an organization called The Village. Our mission is to live out Job 29:12, "Because I rescued the poor who cried for help, and the fatherless who had no one to assist them." We do this by assisting foster families in the greater Atlanta area and in other states across the country where I know foster families. My husband and I are also foster parents and had five different foster children in our home in the last three years. Our foster daughter Emma just went home to her mom after being with us for eighteen months.

This past Christmas I was able to provide more than $15,000 in toys and diapers to foster children through fundraising and donations. I provided Christmas for close to 150 foster children. It was such a huge blessing to be able to take some of the burden off these foster parents. In addition to the Christmas drive, I also provide birthday boxes that include everything you would need to throw a birthday party based on the theme the foster parent gives us along with toys, clothes, and diapers for the foster child. Just these past few months, we have had more than twenty-five requests for birthday boxes. Each box usually contains around

$150 worth of items. I have provided around fifty birthday boxes for foster children this year. These boxes are given to us by individual sponsors or purchased by us using donations sent in by businesses or individuals. We also provide gas cards to foster families (some of them drive more than one hundred miles a day in order to get proper treatment for their children), sponsor extracurricular activities, and anything else a parent would need so their foster child can have a "normal" childhood.

Because of my involvement in foster care and my passion for helping these children, I was recently offered a job as the mentor family program director for a private foster care agency here in Georgia. My boss has encouraged me to continue to provide birthday boxes and Christmas presents to all foster children, regardless of their agency or county. I also run a foster care clothing and donations closet, and I am currently working on scheduling date nights for *all* area foster parents through local churches.

While so much good has come from our obedience to God in our calling as foster parents, I'd be lying if I told you that there is joy in all of it. As foster parents, you are forced to see some of the ugly parts of this world you would never talk about in everyday conversations. You know of the horrific pain and devastation you wouldn't wish upon your worst enemy, much less a precious newborn baby. We have held babies and cried with them as they tried to recover from addiction to horrendous drugs most people wouldn't dare touch. That is why it is so crucial these foster parents, these families, receive the ongoing support and resources that foster agencies are able to provide to them with the help of God's people.

THE JOY OF SUMMER CAMP

RANDY'S STORY

I recently had a home visit with one of the children on my case-load. This particular boy has had behavioral issues since coming into care over a year ago. He refused to bond with his foster mother. He was consistently in trouble at school and daycare. I would go over for a visit, and he would hang his head and not want to interact. He had a very bad attitude in his foster home and had become defiant. And then . . . God.

I literally saw a different child. He was upbeat, smiling and laughing. He had an air of confidence he did not have before. He was so excited to show me his scrapbook from camp and name all the new friends he met. He and his sister even showed me every song and cheer they learned at camp. His foster mother reported he has done a complete 180. She said she knows it was the camp experience and the many prayers said for him. She said she is so glad she didn't give up on him, and I am too. My heart was so full after that visit with him. —Randy, Royal Family KIDS camp counselor

By attending foster care summer camp, some children go fishing in a lake for the first time in their life. Others learn to swim. A boy and a camp counselor chase after a lizard under a nearby rock. Some make jewelry, while others engage in woodworking. Sometimes camp is the greatest week of many of these children's lives. Many do not want to leave, as this week allows them to laugh for perhaps the first time in a long time as they experiencing a week of wonder, joy, and most importantly, unconditional love.

In 1985, Wayne Tesch was serving as an associate pastor at Newport Mesa Church. After a service one Sunday, a woman approached him, asking what he was doing for the foster children of Orange County, California. Pleased by the question, Tesch asked her to talk to several of his Sunday school classes, curious to see what interest there might be from his congregation. Finding little response, the woman again approached Tesch a few weeks later, this time asking him, "What are *you* doing to help them, Pastor Tesch?" As Wayne's educational background was in both Bible and physical education, Wayne decided he would try to put a camp together for foster children in his own town, a camp he called Royal Family Kids Camp.

Now, more than thirty years later, there are 223 Royal Family KIDS camps and thirty-three clubs crisscrossing the globe. Tesch chose the name Royal Family KIDS (RFK) as his wife Diane was captivated by the grandeur of royalty and felt all children deserved to be treated as such. Tesch felt the same, yet he also wanted each child to be part of God's royal family. Along with this, Tesch knew children needed to be loved and accepted by a family.

For foster children, attending the five-day week of camp is a very exciting time. When the six- to twelve-year-old children arrive, they are greeted by warm smiles and heavy cheers from the adult volunteers. Camp counselors hold signs with each child's name on it. For many children, it is better than a red carpet experience. Activities and scheduled group times fill each day. Sadly, for many children, the camp is the first time they may have three cooked meals a day. For some, the most exciting event is the "surprise birthday party" thrown in their honor. This may be the first recognition of a birthday celebrated in their name. For foster parents, it is a five-day respite from care, with a minimal cost for the child to attend.

The camps are sponsored by faith-based organizations that host the weeklong adventure. These organizations connect with and receive the foster children from various social services and child welfare organizations in their area. These faith-based sponsors find a campground to rent for the week, recruit and train adult volunteers who act as counselors and mentors, and raise money to pay for the entire weeklong experience.

Just like Royal Family Kids Camps, there are a number of faith-based summer camps across the nation for children from foster care. To begin with, foster care-based summer camps allow children in care to build on their social skills in a fun and exciting way. As they interact with the other children, their fellow campers, they not only interact with children who may have experienced similar experiences to their own, which might have placed them into care originally, they also have the opportunity to meet children from other cultures and backgrounds. Sharing meals, cabins, and experiences, this is a wonderful way for children who are suffering to build confidence and positive self-esteem.

Foster care camps can offer the opportunity for those siblings and family members who may have been split up during placement to reunite for a week. As they spend time with their brothers and their sisters, they not only build lifelong memories together, they are also reminded they are not alone. Finally, these camps can be a break from the everyday routine and normalcy. With visitations, court hearings, doctor appointments, meetings with therapists and counselors, along with the many challenges that school and everyday life may bring, a vacation at a summer camp is an opportunity for a child in foster care to leave behind all their anxieties, traumas, and all that is foster care, and instead focus on the chance to learn new experiences, have fun, and simply be a kid. Let's look at what some children in foster care say they learned after they attended Journey Weekends in the state of Georgia.

"You can be afraid, but you can also overcome your fears."
"I learned God is always there even if you don't think He is.
He is always gonna be there for us."
"Not to be afraid because God is with you."
"That God is with me no matter what."
"Skills to get along with others."
"I learned that God is always there through the good times and bad."
"I learned about Jesus."
"That God helps you through life every day."

These summer camps offer a number of life-changing and faith-building experiences for these children in need. Churches and faith-based organizations have the opportunity to sponsor camps that may already exist in their area or create new camps where none may exist. What is important to note is this: It is not just the lives of the children who are changed but also the lives of those volunteers who give some of their time to spend with these children in need, children who are longing for someone to pay attention to them, to love them.

MICHELLE'S STORY

My husband and I are foster parents in South Georgia. Almost three years ago, we received a late-night call for the emergency placement of a ten-year-old boy. He had three siblings being sent to other homes. He came around 1 a.m. and was supposed to be a weekend placement until Monday when they could possibly find a home for all four siblings together. All weekend, my husband and I, along with some of our friends, were praying God's will for these children and a home where they could be together. God moved our hearts to turn our three-bedroom house into a five bedroom by putting a wall up in our front living room and making two bedrooms (two boys/two girls). We are a one-income family, so we had no idea how we'd get everything they needed but placed that need in God's hands. We felt without a doubt it was His will to bring them all together in our family.

During that first summer, a group named Called to Care sponsored two of our kiddos to go to Winshape, a program for children in foster care. While there, one of them accepted the Lord as his personal Savior, but it didn't stop there! As he had a visit with his sister, he led her to the Lord. His excitement literally poured over into her life!

The second year, the same group sponsored our kiddos to go to Winshape yet again. This time, during one of the sessions, our fourteen-year-old foster daughter opened up about her life and how she ended up in foster care. As she shared with her peers and the counselors, she forgave her biological dad for the things he had done to her. Each year the children go to Winshape they get so renewed and refreshed. It's wonderful because it shows these children that as a Christian, they can have fun and honor the Lord at the same time. I think it's their favorite week of the year.

QUESTIONS FOR DISCUSSION

What do the words in Psalm 127:3 mean to you?

How did Jesus treat children?

Why was the celebration of his birthday important and life changing to Scotty?

What are some reasons why a child might never celebrate a birthday or Christmas?

What personal traditions do you celebrate on Christmas day?

Share a personal story about a special wrapped present you received as a child either on Christmas morning or on your birthday.

Wayne Tesch was asked by a member of his congregation, "What are *you* doing to help them (children in foster care)?" How would you answer the same question? How would your church answer that same question?

How can a summer camp experience bring healing and hope to a child who has suffered?

Is it important for youth in foster care to be surrounded by people of faith? Why or why not?

One of the youth who attended Journey Weekends spoke of being afraid. What particular fears might a child in foster care experience?

WHEN YOUTH AGE OUT

*B*efore I was a foster parent, I did not understand the heartbreak children in foster care truly suffer. Nor did I understand the heartbreak foster parents go through as well.

Sydney was only seven years old and basically taking care of herself when she joined our family upon being placed into foster care. Both of her parents were missing, and she had been living with her severely alcoholic grandmother. Sydney had to find and prepare her own food each morning and evening, which usually consisted of frozen hot dogs warmed in the microwave. She was also responsible for getting herself ready for school each day.

As a result, she often missed the bus each morning and had a large amount of absences, resulting in her performing at a severely poor level. When the seven-year-old arrived in our home, she had very few academic skills, so much so she could not even write her own name. Her behavior in school was also a challenge, often resulting in meeting with the school principal and myself.

Though Sydney's stay in our home was one filled with many challenges, she had become a valued member of our family during the year-and-a-half she lived with us. She was our daughter, and we loved her. There was no difference between our biological children and Sydney. All were loved the same.

Then two days before Christmas, Sydney left our home and family and moved to a nearby state, as her aunt and uncle had adopted her.

For years, we heard nothing from Sydney, though we prayed for her frequently. Then four years after she had moved from our home, we received a phone call from her one evening.

Picking up the phone that evening, I was met with a familiar voice saying, "Daddy, I want to come home." Instantly recognizing it was Sydney, I was thrilled to speak with her, and both Kelly and I were overjoyed to finally make contact with her. She had been placed into yet another foster home in another state after being bounced from home to home for two years. Speaking to her foster mother at the time of the call, Kelly found out Sydney had run away from her foster home on occasion, had been in a considerable amount of trouble, and had simply become difficult to live with.

Raped, abandoned, moved from home to home, Sydney had lived a life of horror, leaving her in a state of great trauma and anxieties.

Sadly, we were leaving the country that day to visit my wife's family in Australia for three weeks. When we arrived back in the United States, Sydney had already been moved. Despite attempts over and over again by both Kelly and me to locate Sydney, through searches on the Internet, calling up various child welfare agencies in three different states, we met with failure after failure. To be sure, she would probably cause us a great deal of difficulties, but we felt strongly we needed to contact her, to let her know she was thought of, she was loved, she mattered, and she was still part of our family. Yet Sydney was once again lost to us, leaving Kelly and me in grief once more.

Recently, I received a message that she had been located. Five years of looking for her, searching for her, wanting to tell her that she is important, cared for, and loved, I was informed she was located in a children's state mental health facility. The first ten minutes of the phone call I spent with her, I could not hold back the tears. The years of searching for her, only to find her in such a state was surely a mixture of both happiness and grief for me.

It is never too late for a child to start healing and find love. It is never too late to help protect more children and provide a loving place where they can find healing.

My wife and I have visited her often in the mental health hospital. The adults in her life have failed her. The system has failed her. A part of me feels I have failed her. Where do I go from here? Do we adopt her and bring this now eighteen-year-old into our home with the other eight children we have from adoption, foster care, and my own biological children? I do not believe Sydney would be able to function in such a family setting due to the many anxieties she suffers. Do I try and have her moved to our state into a residential group home for girls? Between the states and the foster care system, the rules, regulations, paperwork, and red tape make that very difficult.

Sydney is not doing well. The children's mental health institution has released her, as she is now too old. She is now in her twenties and does not have an education past the ninth grade. Bouncing from one place to another, she is practically homeless.

Again, the foster care system failed Sydney, and it not only grieves me, it drives me each day. I cannot allow this to happen to another child in foster care again. The church and the people of God cannot allow this to happen to any child again.

THE REALITY OF BECOMING TOO OLD FOR FOSTER CARE

For most teenagers in America, turning eighteen years old is an exciting time. High school graduation is right around the corner, and the possibilities of college or an exciting career are on the horizon. A sense of independence often fills the young adult with confidence and enthusiasm. To be sure, it is often seen as a rite of passage into adulthood.

Yet, for roughly 25,000 teens in America each year, turning eighteen in many states is a time filled with anxiety, concern, and, oftentimes, tragedy. For so many the end result is a tragic one.

Typically, children from traditional homes have parents who are able to guide them through these changes, providing help and advice as these eighteen year olds determine the next stage in their lives. Along with this, most young adults are still able to rely on their parents not only for good advice, but for help financially, as well. Foster children, though, do not have these resources, these lifelines so to speak, to help out as they try to ease into their own lives of independence. When they are sick, there is no one to take care of them. Struggling in college? Often, there is no one to help them with their studies. Car broken down? Most former foster children have no one to turn to for help.

Foster youth who age out of care often leave the foster system without the necessary skills, experiences, support, or knowledge they need in order to best adjust to society. Without a family to turn to once they age out, many foster children find themselves in difficult times and situations. According to Chris Chmielewski, an alumni from foster care himself and now editor and owner of *Foster Focus* magazine, "The lack of life skills being taught before a youth aging out of care is seemingly inadequate. Even the most basic of tasks: cleaning laundry, setting up a bank account or finding housing, seem to be foreign concepts to youth leaving care. Without those skills, these kids stand very little chance of not ending up on the streets."

These young adults, who are involuntarily separated from their foster families through the intervention of the government, face higher rates of homelessness, as most have no options for future housing. Unemployment is higher in former foster children, and many struggle financially. This may be due to the fact that roughly 50 percent of those foster youth who age out do not complete high school. Rhonda Sciortino, who also is a foster care alumni, business owner, author, and advocate, stated, "There are an estimated 12 million former foster kids in the US. These survivors of abuse need job skills and employment, job skills that so many do not have."

Even more disturbing is that these youth are more than twice as likely not to have a high school diploma than those their own age. Less than 6 percent of former foster children ever make it to college, let alone graduate with a degree. One third of youth who age out of care seek mental health care. Perhaps more shocking is the that youth who age out of foster care are twice as likely to suffer from Post Traumatic Stress Disorder as US war veterans. Roughly 71 percent of young women who age out of foster care end up pregnant by age twenty-one, and the cycle of foster care continues for the next generation.

Indeed, I have adopted two children from foster care who are third generation foster care. Third generation. Their parents and their grandparents were also in foster care, a system that failed them.

For so many youth, it is a system that fails them and a time of anxiety. It is a system that does not prepare them for a future, and it is a future of tragedy.[12]

Yet there are so many ways today's churches and faith-based groups can help these youth. So many ways God's people can reach out and provide much-needed support and resources to these youth in their very, very desperate time of need. Let me write those four words again: desperate time of need. Those aren't just words I wrote on paper because it sounded nice to my ear. This is reality. Youth aging out of foster care *need* someone to help them or they will become another horrible statistic.

As we have often heard from the pulpit, God gives each of us strengths and talents He expects us to use to further His kingdom on earth by helping others. Let's examine some of that in Scripture.

> EVERY GOOD AND PERFECT GIFT IS FROM ABOVE, COMING DOWN
> FROM THE FATHER OF THE HEAVENLY LIGHTS.
> —JAMES 1:17

> EACH OF YOU SHOULD USE WHATEVER GIFT YOU HAVE RECEIVED
> TO SERVE OTHERS, AS FAITHFUL STEWARDS OF GOD'S GRACE IN ITS
> VARIOUS FORMS. IF ANYONE SPEAKS, THEY SHOULD DO SO AS ONE
> WHO SPEAKS THE VERY WORDS OF GOD. IF ANYONE SERVES, THEY
> SHOULD DO SO WITH THE STRENGTH GOD PROVIDES, SO THAT IN
> ALL THINGS GOD MAY BE PRAISED THROUGH JESUS CHRIST.
> TO HIM BE THE GLORY AND THE POWER FOR EVER AND EVER. AMEN.
> —1 PETER 4:10–11

> THERE ARE DIFFERENT KINDS OF SERVICE, BUT THE SAME LORD.
> THERE ARE DIFFERENT KINDS OF WORKING, BUT IN ALL OF THEM
> AND IN EVERYONE IT IS THE SAME GOD AT WORK.
> —1 CORINTHIANS 12:5–6

> FOR BY THE GRACE GIVEN ME I SAY TO EVERY ONE OF YOU: DO NOT
> THINK OF YOURSELF MORE HIGHLY THAN YOU OUGHT, BUT RATHER
> THINK OF YOURSELF WITH SOBER JUDGMENT, IN ACCORDANCE WITH
> THE FAITH GOD HAS DISTRIBUTED TO EACH OF YOU. FOR JUST AS
> EACH OF US HAS ONE BODY WITH MANY MEMBERS, AND THESE
> MEMBERS DO NOT ALL HAVE THE SAME FUNCTION, SO IN CHRIST
> WE, THOUGH MANY, FORM ONE BODY, AND EACH MEMBER BELONGS

TO ALL THE OTHERS. WE HAVE DIFFERENT GIFTS, ACCORDING TO
THE GRACE GIVEN TO EACH OF US. IF YOUR GIFT IS PROPHESYING,
THEN PROPHESY IN ACCORDANCE WITH YOUR FAITH; IF IT IS
SERVING, THEN SERVE; IF IT IS TEACHING, THEN TEACH; IF IT IS
TO ENCOURAGE, THEN GIVE ENCOURAGEMENT; IF IT IS GIVING,
THEN GIVE GENEROUSLY; IF IT IS TO LEAD, DO IT DILIGENTLY;
IF IT IS TO SHOW MERCY, DO IT CHEERFULLY.
—ROMANS 12:3–8

15 WAYS TO HELP A YOUTH AGING OUT OF CARE

1. Become a tutor or mentor

Yet another sobering statistic about foster care is 50 percent of children in foster care will drop out of school. Only 2.5 percent will graduate from college with a four-year degree.

Why is this? Why do so many children from foster care drop out of school? Quite simply, school has failed these children. As they bounce from home to home through multiple displacements, a child not only loses trust in others and develops issues of attachment, he also falls further and further behind in school. When he finally ages out of the system, he is often anxious to quit school.

We all know that in today's world, if one does not have at the very least a high school diploma, or a General Education Development (GED) Certificate of High School Equivalency, than there is very little chance that he will be able to acquire a job of any kind. Youth in foster care need to stay in school, and today's church can help them do just that. Volunteers from your church can help these children by volunteering as tutors who can also act as a much needed cheerleading squad for the youth in foster care, cheering on each success in class and in school and helping them during those times of difficulty or failure.

2. Donate school supplies or sponsor a student.

As we have seen, there are many challenges preventing children in foster care from succeeding in school. One way to reverse this disturbing and harmful trend is to help children in care with school supplies. By donating paper, pencils, pens, notebooks, rulers, calculators, and school bags to foster children, foster parents, your local foster parent associations, or to the area's child welfare agency, you are not only able to help both the child and the foster parents. You can also help by sponsoring a child in a school sport by paying for entry fees and equipment, a child in the marching band by paying any fees and for their uniform or instrument, or any child with related club and organization fees. The more support a child has while in school, the better equipped they are to stay in school and succeed.

3. Develop a college scholarship fund.
One of the reasons former foster kids have such a hard time receiving a four-year degree is they simply cannot afford to attend college. Your church, your faith-based group, and your organization can help with a college scholarship fund.

I recently spoke to a private foster care agency in California about the dangers of aging out of foster care. One of the caseworkers at the agency told me how they help by awarding a college scholarship of $5,000 each year to a foster child in their area who has shown commitment in school and is hoping to further their education. By creating a college scholarship fund for those youth in foster care in your area, you are helping to not only send a foster child to college, you are also helping to keep them off the streets and out of jail.

4. Teach money skills and the importance of saving.
Recently, I helped en eighteen-year-old teenager from foster care in our home open up his first bank account. He had acquired his first paying job working at the town's dry cleaning store and was earning money for the first time in his life. He was excited, to say the least, and I was excited for him. He was so excited, he wanted to go and spend all the money he earned right away! I could just envision him leaving our home and the foster care system, spending all his money and not having any money for the essentials in life—food, water, rent, electricity, transportation, and the reality of everyday bills and expenses. This is one reason why so many youth end up homeless and on the streets. They just do not know how to save or properly manage their money.

I am not a great money manager. My wife is, so she handles all the bills. She is the expert in our house. There may be great money managers and experts in your own church or organization who can teach children in foster care the importance of money management and why it is necessary to save up for the proverbial rainy day. Each child needs to learn how to save money and manage it wisely. By sitting down with children in foster care, even at a young age, and helping them develop strong money management skills, you are helping to provide them some of the keys to success later on in life.

6. Donate household goods to a local foster care agency.

It can be a difficult time when a young person first moves out and starts life on their own. Building a life and building a home can be a challenge. For those who have little money and little resources, these challenges can be even more daunting. One way to help a foster youth as he ages out is to lend a helping hand with some of these so-called simple items. With the donation of pots, pans, plates, cups, silverware, and other necessary and simple household items to your local foster care agency, they can be placed in the hands of those youth who are in desperate need, yet do not have the finances to pay for these household goods. Cleaning items such as laundry detergent, dishwashing soap, toilet cleaner, etc. can also help tremendously for someone who is just trying to get on their feet and begin the journey of adulthood with a positive step forward.

7. Donate furniture and clothing to local foster care agency.

Whether it is casual clothing, sleep wear, coats, jackets, undergarments, or other attire, those who are trying to survive day-to-day on their own will need clothing. Imagine what a nice set of clothing would do for someone who has only the clothes on his back, yet has a job interview scheduled at a respectable business. Churches and nonprofits can host their own clothes drive for youth who age out and donate the collected clothing to their local foster care agency or association.

Furniture items can also be collected and donated. Chairs, couches, beds, tables are all items many of us take for granted. Yet for the young adult who has little to no money, and little to no support, these pieces of furniture can be terribly difficult to come by. Whether it is brand new or slightly and gently used, furniture can go a long way in filling an important need for a young adult struggling to start out.

8. Teach the importance of good health and hygiene.

A while back, we had a seventeen-year-old homeless boy come live with us. For his entire life, Michael suffered great emotional abuse and neglect from his mother. Bouncing around from one home to another with his mother and her numerous boyfriends, the mother never truly had time for him and never took time to teach what most would consider to be the very basics of life. She too suffered from her own emotional challenges and instability and was not equipped to be a parent to her only son. The mother's boyfriends, who came in and out of their homes, either ignored him or verbally and physically abused him. When Michael was sixteen years old, the mother's newest boyfriend, who the mother had met a month prior, moved into the home and gave the mother an ultimatum—her boyfriend of one month or her sixteen-year-old son. I imagine you can quickly determine who the mother chose.

Michael found himself homeless later that afternoon. He spent a year with a very abusive and manipulative family, who did him further harm both emotionally and physically, and spent a short time in the local jail on false charges. My wife Kelly and I received a phone call from the local sheriff, who was also a friend of mine, asking if we would take Michael into our home for the next nine months, until the teenager could graduate from school. As we were still grieving a failed adoption from foster care just two months prior, along with the fact that my wife had been suffering from her daily battle with Lyme disease, I was unsure if this was the right time for us to take another child into our home. Kneeling together by our bed, Kelly and I turned to God in prayer, looking for direction. When we finished, Kelly turned to look at me, a slight smile beginning to appear on her face.

"We have no choice; we have to take him into our home. He can't stay another moment in jail," she told me. An hour later, I sat across from him and a deputy in the county jail, inviting him to come and live with me and my family.

Michael was incredibly bright, loved to read, and excelled in school. Yet he struggled immensely with social and basic living skills.

I found myself teaching this seventeen-year-old young man the same things I was teaching my youngest, four-year-old daughter. Despite his book knowledge and school smarts, the homeless youth needed to be taught basic health and hygiene lessons like brushing his teeth after meals, combing his hair, how to clean himself properly in a shower, using deodorant, and even how to use a toilet.

The sad reality is that there are far too many youth like Michael who have never had someone teach them these very basic living skills. Churches, volunteers, and faith-based groups can not only teach youth in foster care these valuable yet simple lessons, as well as offer classes, but they can also donate such items as soap, shampoo, conditioner, deodorant, toothbrushes, toothpaste, combs and brushes, and other hygiene items to foster care agencies and foster parent associations in your area.

9. Teach and maintain good eating habits.

My wife is a doctor of nutrition. In our home, it is all things organic and healthy—nothing processed. For myself? Well, I am a dyed-in-the-wool devoted lover of frozen pizzas, chocolate chip cookies, and Fruity Pebbles cereal. Make no mistake; my wife's world and my own often collide!

Yet, through the years, I have come to truly appreciate, understand, and value not only my wife's dedication to healthy eating for all in our household but also the importance of it. I have watched child after child come to live with us who have come from environments where they did not eat healthy and who had suffered terribly from malnutrition or not having the right things to eat. As my wife would prepare them healthy meals, chocked full of fruits and vegetables, many of the children did not recognize some of the food placed in front of them.

Malnutrition can hinder a child's ability to grow normally, as well as impede brain, behavior, and weight development. Their underdeveloped immune systems make them more prone to infections. As my wife Dr. Kelly would tell you, most processed foods have little nutritional value and contain white sugars, white flours, artificial sweeteners, or food colorings, often leaving a body weak. Many children in foster care have never had the opportunity to eat healthy or been taught the importance of doing so. Through workshops, individual lessons, and mentoring, faith-based groups have the opportunity to teach the importance of good nutrition, how to read food labels, and how to choose nutritional foods.

10. Teach cooking skills.
Cooking is an important life skill. It is an art. It is also fun. What many do not realize is that it is also a wonderful opportunity for youth ministry.

As anyone with a teenager in their house knows, teens love to eat. They eat while watching TV, they eat while playing video games, they eat while talking on the phone and texting their friends—they just eat all the time. For those parents who have children away at college, military, etc., when they come back home for a visit, they eat everything in the fridge and pantry. They pretty much depend upon you, the parent, to provide them their favorite food, whether it is a freshly cooked homemade meal or some sort of snack food wrapped up in a potato chip and cookie package.

For those youth who age out of foster care and are on their own, there is usually little chance of them getting a home-cooked meal. And many youth in care do not have the cooking skills needed in order to simply prepare a meal, let alone one that is healthy and nutritious. Fortunately, many churches have opened up their own church kitchens, using both food and cooking as not only a service to youth in foster care but also as a faith-based ministry program. While teaching youth the fundamentals of cooking and giving children in foster care both courses and classes, accompanied by hands-on practice, these ministry programs also weave in biblical lessons. These churches and faith-based groups are also opening up possible career options for youth as they discover the joy of cooking.

11. Be a transport/driver to youth who have aged out.
It should come as no surprise that most youth who age out of foster care do not have a driver's license or any method of transportation available to them. Without transportation, an aged-out teen faces the risk of not being able to succeed on many levels. Whether it is getting to a job interview, meeting with a military recruiter, going to the grocery store, meeting with a mentor, getting to work, or visiting

a doctor or hospital when sick, transportation helps make all that happen.

Perhaps your church or faith-based organization can arrange some sort of transportation ministry. Perhaps some sort of modern-day, faith-based Uber or taxi system—free of charge, of course. Furthermore, there may be some in your church or faith-based group who may be even willing to provide driving lessons, including how to carve out independence in this fashion.

12. If you own a business, provide discounts on goods and services.
One way to simply begin ministering to anyone in need is to start where you are, with what you have. During my own fifteen years as a foster parent, I have seen this wonderful act of giving and of faith help children, as well as the foster parents, time and time again. There is a lovely lady in my town who gives free haircuts to children in foster care. Our doctor places children in foster care at the top of her list each time one is sick and comes into the doctor's office. Another person offers free art lessons. What a wonderful opportunity for people of faith to share their God-given talents and skills to children in foster care. Whether it is with carpentry, music lessons, dance, or even auto mechanics for foster parents, members of the faith community have countless ways to help children in care, those who age out, and those who care for the children, by not only offering their skills and talents, but at the same time, helping in a financial way.

13. If you own a business, consider training and hiring former foster youth.
Bryant has owned his own business for over ten years now. When he first started out, he struggled like so many small time business owners do. It took him a few years to become financially stable in his business, crediting an older member of his church for stepping in and acting as a mentor of sorts. Now Bryant does the same thing and has recently hired a young adult who has aged out of foster care to help him.

Like Bryant, business owners, whether big or small, have the opportunity to help alumni from foster care, as well as youth still currently placed into foster homes, by providing them jobs. When hiring someone who was in foster care, you are sending them a number of lessons. To begin with, when someone, perhaps like you, hires a youth in foster care, you are sending him a powerful message that he matters, that he has value, and that he has something to offer. The gift of a job allows youth in foster care to have a sense of self worth and helps them develop lessons in responsibility and time and money management. Along with this, important job skills can be learned, and maybe even a career path for the youth to follow. You are helping to lower the homelessness rate as the young adult begins to earn money honestly through good ole hard work. With a job, new job skills, and a sense of self worth, you may help to bring an end to the generational cycle of foster care for that young adult.

14. Be a mentor, and teach important social and communication skills.

Years ago, there was a wonderful person in my church by the name of Kris, who was a mentor to Marie, an eight-year-old child from foster care who was placed in our home. Kris would meet with Marie every week. Sometimes they would meet at church, other times it might be at our house, still other times, it might be at the local ice cream parlor. Some days, Kris would help Marie with some schoolwork, as Marie was struggling in school. Other times, Kris might bring some Bible-based crossword puzzles with her. Kris also taught Marie some simple lessons in sewing and arts and crafts. Other times, the two would just sit down over some bowls full of ice cream and chat together. Not only was Kris helping Marie with school work, teaching her arts and crafts, or treating her to some ice cream, this mentor for our eight-year-old daughter from foster care was giving weekly lessons in communication and social skills, skills the troubled child severely lacked. To me, these were much more valuable than helping her catch up in math or reading or introducing her to a new arts and crafts project.

Today's faith-based members have the opportunity to help a youth in foster care build strong social and communication skills simply by spending time with them. For many of these youth who are in care, there have been few, if any, adults who have spent time in helping the child develop social skills, skills they will surely need once they age out. Many youth in foster care do not know how to introduce themselves, express their emotions and feelings when upset or frustrated, or even look someone in the eye. It is important for children to learn socialization skills in school and at home.

Children with poor communication and social skills are less likely to develop healthy and positive relationships later as they grow to adulthood. Furthermore, those with poor skills tend to have a higher likelihood of getting into trouble with the law, and even turn to a life of crime. Whether these social and communication skills help them with a job, in the classroom, in their day-to-day interaction with others, or just stay out of trouble, far too often, youth in care lack these important skills. As we both know, without strong, healthy, positive social and communication skills, it is terribly difficult to not only succeed in life but simply to survive.

15. Be a friend, willing to listen and willing to help.
Take time to simply listen. That is what youth in foster care often need and want. Though their stories might be sad, shocking, disturbing, and tragic, they need to talk about their feelings, and they need someone to listen to them.

Now, I must be honest with you. I have cried while listening to the stories from the children and youth in foster care in my own home. Some of the stories are so heart wrenching, so tragic, so disturbing, that my heart breaks from the realization that these children have suffered such crimes against them. I imagine you very well may cry as well. I am here to tell you that it is okay. It is okay to cry. Your tears and your broken heart are a sign of validation to them that what they have suffered is indeed painful. At the same time, your tears are also a sign that somebody cares for them. Sure, have a box of tissues nearby. Place a reassuring hand on their shoulder. Offer them a hug if they ask for one. By simply listening, you are giving them a great gift. You may be the first person who has shown interest in them and is willing to let them share their story. Your listening ear tells them they matter.

QUESTIONS FOR DISCUSSION

How did the foster care system fail Sydney?

What might happen to a child who never feels loved?

How does 1 Corinthians 12:4–8 apply to how we are to share our love with children in need?

Why might a youth from foster care who has aged out quit school? How has the school system failed him?

What challenges to young adults who have no support system or education face where you live?

When you were first on your own, what challenges and struggles did you face? How might it be more difficult for youth in foster care when they age out of the system?

Before Michael moved into the author's home after being kicked out of the house by his mother at age sixteen, there was no one who taught him even the most basic of skills. What does Proverbs 22:6 say about the importance of how we teach our children and how we raise them?

What businesses in your own area can your church or faith-based group approach and ask about helping with discounted goods and services for youth in foster care who have aged out?

Why do youth in foster care need someone to simply listen to them?

What form of outreach and ministry can your church do to help youth who have aged out of foster care in your own area?

BEING AN ADVOCATE

For months now, the two foster parents had been taking care of three foster children in their home, as well as their own two children. Of the three foster siblings, two of them were infants, aged six months and eighteen months, while the third was a seven-year-old. All three were challenging in their own way; the baby was born addicted to meth, the eighteen-month-old showed signs of reactive attachment disorder, and the seven-year-old was struggling academically and behaviorally in school. The three foster children took all the foster parents' time, including nights, as the baby slept fitfully. The parents were unable to devote much time to their own eleven and thirteen-year-old. After five months with the three children, the foster parents were worn out, exhausted, and in need of a break. Along with this, there was a wedding the family wanted to attend, though it was out of state. As they were not permitted to take the three foster children over state lines, they placed the three in respite care for the weekend, taking their own two children with them to the wedding, a time they needed for themselves.

Respite care refers to one foster family caring for another family's foster children for a short amount of time. This type of foster care is especially helpful when foster children have behaviors typically seen in many therapeutic foster homes.

Respite can be used for a variety of reasons. A foster family may need to attend to a family emergency of some kind and may not have the ability, opportunity, or permission to take the foster child with them. Take for example a foster family of one foster child and a biological child of their own. There is a death in the family, and they have to travel outside the state with only one day's notice. As the foster child has severe social challenges and disabilities, it is deemed by both the foster family and the child welfare agency that a funeral is neither a healthy nor appropriate environment for the child. As a result, the child is placed in a respite home with another foster family during that time.

Another foster family needs to place their foster child into respite for several weeks as the foster mother battles an illness. As the foster father is often away at work, the foster mother is unable to properly care for the child during this time, and the child is placed into another home in the community. During this time, the original foster family remains in constant contact with the child through phone calls and occasional visits with the child in the respite provider's home, as well as taking the child out to eat nearby. By doing so, it helps ensure the bonds of attachment, security, and love they created with the child are not separated during the respite placement.

There are those times, of course, when foster families simply become exhausted, or "burned out," if you will. Perhaps the foster child has been in the home for an extended period of time and the family has grown mentally, emotionally, and physically weary from care. This is a very real possibility, one that should not be ignored for the health of all involved. In order for the family to remain not only healthy foster parents but also a healthy family unit, they may need a break from care, an opportunity to "recharge their batteries" and focus on their own family unit, lest it begin to suffer from exhaustion and lack of attention. This helps foster parent retention, as foster parents feel that they can continue to care for children in their home and face the challenges, after a little break.

Julia's Story

——— ◦ ———

This is our story of respite at the right moment. We had our foster daughter, Niza, for eighteen months. Her mom had passed away due to complications from surgery while dad was still an addict and unable to complete his case plan. We had an amazing relationship with her maternal grandparents, and all of us hoped we would be able to adopt her soon. My heart, though, always had a small reserve, like a whisper to my soul that she was not going to be with us forever. I now believe it was God trying to prepare me for her going to another family.

My coworkers were all trying to win a radio station trip to Las Vegas. I flippantly joked that if we didn't get to keep Niza, I'd want to lick my wounds in Vegas. I never enter contests, I never even win at scratch tickets. But when I dialed the number, I actually won the trip. The next week at court, the caseworker had found the brother of Niza's biological father (they were never told she was in foster care, but that she was instead living with her biological mom's parents). I felt guilty, confused, and angry, but it is the law for reunification.

We had never used our respite hours we were granted as foster parents, so this seemed like the right time, as she was transitioning over to her family (they would eventually legally adopt her—giving her a forever mommy and daddy). We used another foster mom who was wonderful with Niza, and the trip to Las Vegas helped remind me and my husband that we needed time. Even though our hearts were breaking, God had heard my "joke" and agreed we needed the time alone together.

Niza's new parents are wonderful with her. They wanted to continue a relationship with us, but due to Niza's age and the fact she called us mommy and daddy, we prayed on it and felt she needed to bond with them and them alone. I love my little girl and pray for her happiness every day. She is on the path God needs her to be on. I will always be grateful respite was there to allow me and my husband to step out of the moment and be there for each other.

THE POWER OF A CASA

I am here to tell you that I love CASAs!

Court Appointed Special Advocates, otherwise known as CASAs, are volunteers who are appointed by a court or by a judge to help children in foster care. These volunteers advocate for the best interests of the child in court and serve these children in a number of ways. To begin with they gather information, documents, and records for court. They spend time listening to the child and family members, getting to know the child's concerns and needs. CASAs appear in court and advocate for the child's best interests as they help those in court better understand the child and their needs, providing testimony when necessary. Another important part of being a CASA is recommending the appropriate and helpful services for the child and making sure the child's case plan is being followed. In fact, you do not need to be a lawyer, judge, or even a social worker to be a Court Appointed Special Advocate. You simply need to have a desire to help a child in foster care by giving a few hours of your time each week.

Over the years, I have had a few CASAs serve as advocates for some of the children from foster care in my own home. I say some as, unfortunately, there have only been six CASAs for my fifty-plus children. Why? Well, there are not enough CASAs in my area. There are not enough people willing to volunteer to help these children in need or perhaps not enough people who are familiar with what a Court Appointed Special Advocate is. In fact, I would not be surprised if you had never heard of the CASA program. Most people of faith I have spoken with are unfamiliar with it. Yet, it is a program that is so very important, as well as so very helpful for children in foster care.

Becoming a CASA volunteer takes only a few hours a week, but it could make a vital difference in your community. The church, likewise, could further their own work with the foster care system by encouraging or organizing volunteers willing to undergo CASA training. Consider the steps toward such a goal for yourself or your congregation today.

Finally, let's look at what it means to be a CASA from someone who has been serving in that capacity since 2009.

Olga's Story

It was hard to make the decision to become a CASA. My main fear, as is the fear of all of us who volunteer, was to become so emotionally involved with the children I would be serving that I would want to adopt them all and fail at being practical in my recommendations to the court. As it turns out, no matter how much I would want to take these children home with me, they all want their own parents. That bond is so strong it defeats neglect and maltreatment.

CASA training was incredibly effective at helping me realize children who enter the foster care system have suffered and their suffering is best treated by professionals. Their needs go beyond my capabilities. But it also trained me well to understand my role was to be a significant vessel to help the court system understand the child's circumstances better and ensure all their needs were met by presenting the judge with facts and solid recommendations.

As a CASA volunteer, I get the opportunity to meet these wonderful, beautiful children and give them one thing they are desperately needing: consistency. I have the time, so I make it a priority to set up frequent visits. By seeing a friendly face that over the weeks slowly becomes familiar, the children learn that you're not going away, so you must care. And when they realize you do care about them they learn to trust you. That gift of trust alone is the biggest key to halting the cycle of abuse. It is a catalyst that teaches them there are other options and that life can be better.

One of my earliest cases was a young girl who kept running away from her grandmother's home. She either went to a neighbor's house and snuck into their basement to sleep or slept on park benches. She was being evaluated for bipolar disorder and had already received the diagnosis of oppositional defiant disorder and reactive attachment disorder. A psychiatric evaluation was ordered, along with quite a few medications.

Even though she did not say a word for our first four visits, I learned she liked to color and paint. Every week I brought coloring books, small canvases, and acrylic paints. Slowly she began coming out of her shell and eventually learned to tolerate me. One day the grandmother was being especially harsh with her criticism and complaints, which I very quickly put a stop to. I reminded the grandmother I was there for her granddaughter and to make sure her needs were met regardless of what the general opinion about her behavior was. I saw a significant change in the girl's demeanor from that day forward. You see, nobody had ever stood up for her. Nobody had paid attention to what she liked or had taken the time to be reliable and consistent.

After nearly three months of visits she finally decided to trust me, and that trust enabled her to feel safe enough to confide in me she was being sexually molested by her grandmother's boyfriend. Worse yet, her grandmother knew.

I'm happy to report a wonderful and loving family eventually adopted her. She's a senior in high school and captain of the cheerleading squad. But what would have happened if no one had taken the time to be consistent and show her what trust looked and felt like? She and I remain close friends to this day.

So if you were wondering if taking a few hours out of your week to advocate for a child in foster care can really make a difference, now you know. It does. You can change a child's life. Is there a better job than that?

Questions for Discussion

Jesus spent time by Himself, as Scripture tells us in Luke 5:15–16. Why do foster parents need to take time for themselves?

What is respite care?

Why might respite care be important for foster parents?

How could your church create a respite care program?

What is a CASA?

How can a CASA fulfill the words in Matthew 5:16?

How did Olga find fulfillment as a CASA?

Why might serving as a CASA be fruitful for some members of your church or faith-based organization?

Alumni Stories

*O*ver the years, I have met countless alumni from the foster care system who have been changed by those who cared for them, found healing through those who have been led by faith to help them, and become successful in many areas because someone cared enough to help them. I have sat across the table from many alumni who have told me, with tears of joy in their eyes, how a church member or a faith-filled foster parent changed their life. I have spoken on the phone and interviewed dozens of former foster youth who have shared with me how they have healed from their abuse and trauma due to someone sharing acts of kindness, prayer, and the love of God with them.

I have seen so many of my own children from foster care age out of the system and lead healthy, positive, and productive lives due in part because people in my own church felt called to help them in some fashion. We have seen throughout this book how people of faith can help youth in foster care in a number of ways.

I need to remind you of something important, though. We often do not see God's plan being carried out, as you no doubt know. God's timing is perfect, and we may not see how our Loving Father is working inside a child in foster care. Yet, what is also important to remember is there is a very real chance that in the future, the foster child you helped may not come to know your name. There is a good chance that in the future, the foster child you cared for in some way will never recognize your face. But I can assure you each foster child you, your church, or your faith-based organization helps in some fashion will remember one thing later on in life. They will remember that for a period in his life, he was loved, and some day down the road, he will blossom into something better because of it. When you share your faith and God's love with a child in need, you are changing the life of a child and changing the world. You are answering God's call to serve Him and His children in need.

As I was working on this book, I had the privilege and blessing to hear from many alumni from foster care. So many of them wanted to share their own personal stories with you and wanted you to know how a person or organization of faith helped them and how their lives have been changed by the grace and love of God.

Shay's Story

My name is Shay Sorrells, and I was in foster care from the age of five until my eighteenth birthday. I lived in all types of placements, including foster homes, a group home, and relative care throughout my time in care. I became involved with church during high school. I made some friends at a birthday party who invited me to a church youth group to play on their sports teams. I didn't know churches had sports teams, and after moving to so many schools and being afraid of moving again, I didn't want to join the regular school team, so this was a safe option. The teams played in tournaments hosted at colleges and churches throughout the state. Through some interesting turn of events I ended up applying at several of those colleges my senior year. I had never really believed I would be college bound. My high school teachers had been pretty clear I wasn't college material, and I didn't have the writing skills. They were unaware of my life outside school. The youth group leader was one of the few people who told me I could go to college. I would have to work hard, but I could make it happen.

Unfortunately, my high school grades weren't stellar, I hadn't taken the SATs or ACTs, and I really didn't even know how to approach the process of applying for colleges. The youth leaders at the church helped me start looking and attending college fairs. I started getting calls and materials from all the schools, and it was overwhelming. I was working hard to take extra classes in math and history to meet minimum requirements. Then I got a call from an admission counselor at what is now known as Vanguard University of Southern California, a small private Christian college. The counselor helped me with every step of the application and financial aid process. He listened and was open to helping me problem solve. I was conditionally accepted, but I needed to take the SATs, and it was May of my senior year. I signed up for the last possible test, and it was canceled the day of due to a fire. I figured college was never meant to be, and I effectively gave up. But my counselor was not so willing to throw in the towel. He went to the dean and was able to get me a waiver. If I started with basic math and English and a college basics course, I could attend in the fall.

But there were still obstacles to overcome as I struggled with taking tests and retaining information in my classes. But a professor helped me figure out I had a processing/learning disorder that had gone unnoticed. He taught me some techniques and offered test options, such as reading it aloud for me. Another of my professors also read my tests aloud and offered me options to discuss materials in a smaller setting. I began to excel. If I had not been at a small Christian college with no more than twenty students in a class, I do not think I would have had these options. I graduated four years later with my BA in psychology.

I was also able to get involved in a local ministry on campus and at the church adjacent to our campus. I became a junior high mentor, which lead to a summer job helping run summer camps. I had a place to stay and income to support me. I became great friends with the youth pastors and their extended family as well as the families of the youth I mentored.

Shortly after graduating, I had no place to live, and one of the families of the youth I mentored took me in. I lived with them, and in my heart consider them one of the best foster homes (though I was twenty-one and totally out of care) I ever had. I actually ended up staying with families who were all from that church or from that school for the next several years until I was married. I learned so much about marriage, parenting, faith, and life staying with these families. They all took me in and loved on me (as much as I would allow). What I realized is I was ready. I had done some healing and worked through some of my trauma. I was ready to learn about family.

I have contact with all the people in my story to this day. They are my chosen family. I would not be where I am at now if not for God placing them in my life and helping me. I am now a chief program officer at a national nonprofit that oversees prevention and promotion services in affordable housing. I earned my master of social work in 2009 and began my doctorate in social work at the University of Southern California this year.

I advocate whenever possible for foster youth to attend small private colleges, for people to mentor and love on them, and for them to get involved in churches and for churches to get involved with them. I truly believe the miserable statistics of foster youth graduating college with degrees could greatly be impacted through the church's involvement, just like in my own life and my own story.

Jamie's Story

My personal journey through foster care demonstrates the opportunity foster care can bring to a child. I grew up in a life destined for failure. Born in a small town in Kansas, my parents were poor, addicted to drugs, and were heavy alcoholics. They battled depression while suffering from other mental health issues. My father committed suicide after losing a battle with severe depression and alcoholism. My mother routinely placed my younger brother and me in dangerous situations as young children. From the time I was born until I was eighteen years old, I moved more than twenty times between my biological parents, grandparents, and the foster care system. However, being placed into foster care saved my life.

I was placed into foster care in a small town in Kansas. This small town provided me a new opportunity to succeed. It also saved my life by introducing me to Jesus Christ. My first foster family taught me the importance of faith and shared with me how to accept Jesus into my heart. I was saved and baptized while in foster care. The entire community embraced the challenge of supporting my growth and assisting me on my path to knowing and understanding God. In fact, I have penned three books on foster care and have dedicated each book to that community. One of those books—*Finding Your Hero*—was written to demonstrate to the world just how special this community is. Each character represents a real-life person. I can't say enough about the people in this community.

Moreover, this community provided me a strong foundation to succeed. At the age of seventeen, I enlisted in the United States Army Reserve. After 9/11, I deployed to the Middle East in support of Operation Enduring Freedom and Operation Iraqi Freedom. It was only through the strength of God, for which foster care brought to me, that I made it through and survived deployment in an austere environment.

I continue to serve our great country. As a major in the United States Army, I have traveled the world and served in numerous capacities. I have served as a commander for more than four hundred soldiers, served on the Army staff at the Pentagon, trained in Germany with the German Armed Forces, launched one of the largest continuous process improvement programs in the Army Reserve, and much more.

If it were not for my time as a foster child, I would not be where I am today. Foster care has provided me a platform to share my story. It has provided me with an insatiable thirst for growth and success. Foster care has also provided me with a mission. This mission is to improve the current system, as more children should have the experience I had. As a trained problem solver, I have launched numerous improvement efforts to achieve this, including a television show, books and blogs, and a doctoral dissertation.

Foster children do not have parents who either know how or are able to provide them a life filled with opportunity. This is where the foster care system has the opportunity to play a vital role. These kids need a strong system, because when it is done right, they can succeed. In fact, a former foster child once told me she viewed foster care as a prestigious scholarship for college. This is the type of mindset all children should have. Foster care can save the life of a child, just as it did for me. When I think back to my time in foster care, I am amazed by the people who came to my rescue. I know meeting them was not merely a coincidence . . . they were placed in my life for a specific reason. God placed them in my life to save me, yet they still had to answer the call. Think of the possibilities if everyone answered the call. Think of all the lives that would be saved.

Elena's Story

I was first placed into foster care when I was fifteen years old, a victim of sexual abuse, and aged out of the system when I was twenty-one years old. I was able to choose the first foster care placement at the DFCS office. It was a week from my sixteenth birthday and I was in the ninth grade. I didn't know how long I would be at that placement. There were other foster children placed in the home—one had even been adopted by the family. The others had suffered a form of abuse or had a parent in prison.

I would often do my homework on the kitchen counter while my foster mom cooked. I talked, she listened. We celebrated birthdays, went shopping, and took pictures as a family, trying to feel normal.

After two years, I was placed out of the region, out from the school I attended, and away from the people I had been surrounded by. Three years after leaving, I was surprised to hear from that first placement. I was invited back into their home and in their new church they were pastoring. It was Christmastime, and we each had lots of gifts from our county's DFCS office, so it was a morning of opening presents and being around people.

While a part of the foster care system, I wasn't able to go home or have home visits due to my history of sexual abuse. After I aged out at twenty-one, I went to live in an assisted living home. I recently reconnected once again to my first foster family placement, and we continue to talk to this day.

Donetia's Story

I'm a Baby Boomer. My seventeen-year ordeal with the nation's largest foster care system in California began in the late 50s, when I was eleven months old, with my older brother by my side. He and I were the oldest of what would eventually be nine siblings. Over the years, I had the privilege of sharing time and space with four foster families as well as several months in a group home for girls. One of my foster placements was led by a husband and wife who professed and practiced a lifestyle of Christian service, faith, and belief in everyday life.

My initiation into the world of heartbreak and shattered dreams occurred the day I was separated from my brother, who went to live in another foster home. Our separation occurred when my brother was ten or eleven. My brother didn't like the household chores we were assigned on weekends, the evenings we spent in front of a chalkboard being drilled on math and spelling by our foster father, or the restrictions and physical punishment that came with misbehaving.

I don't know how I managed to suppress or repress for so many years the unspoken trauma that occurred when we were separated from our birth mother, but I found myself having to do whatever it was I did again and again, day in and day out, especially with my brother's departure.

My brother's absence as a protector and elder sibling opened the door to years of sexual abuse and molestation by my foster parent's biological son and other males living in our home. To this day, I have no regrets about the events that transpired during my youth. This is because I forgave myself for not having the courage to tell my foster parents or the self-esteem to resist the unwanted advances of my brothers. I forgave my foster parents for their inadvertent lack of oversight about unknown events. I have no regrets because I know the power of forgiveness. By practicing forgiveness and clinging to my faith, I've experienced healing and restoration of every breach and broken wall in my life. Only the love of God and the real-life manifestation of His grace could erase a memory bank filled with deposits of pain, hurt, and trauma.

My graduation from high school at sixteen triggered a removal from my fourth foster placement. I had no idea I wouldn't be able to stay in foster care if I were no longer attending school. The hunt for an alternative placement led to a brief stay in juvenile hall, which made no sense. I wasn't incorrigible, guilty of truancy, or a juvenile delinquent.

My transfer from juvenile hall to a group home for girls turned out to be a huge blessing. While unpacking my belongings and placing them in storage cabinets in the room I had been assigned, I found a copy of the Bible. I used the blank pages between books of the Bible to write love letters to God. I didn't have a church home or place of worship, but I firmly believed my dream of living a better life would one day come true.

After living in the group home for about eight months, the owners invited me to live in their home. In their words, "I didn't fit the profile of the girls ordered by the court to stay in the home." When I turned eighteen, the owners, a Christian couple, adopted me and set me on a path to cultivating a life grounded in faith, service, and good works.

The first person to affirm my purpose in life was a lawyer and Sunday school teacher who inspired a love for learning, which overflowed into a passion for serving others by sharing insight, wisdom, and knowledge. My adopted mom affirmed my ability to encourage, mentor, and coach others, while my adopted dad became a source of peace, calm, and protection.

The life lessons taught by my mentors, adopted parents, and other Christian role models became the foundation for rising above the mediocrity, obscurity, and musings of life as a foster child. My mentors inspired me to embrace my gifts and talents. They strengthened me and taught me how to rise above the chaos, confusion, and war that rages within the heart and mind of those who have been abused, abandoned, or neglected. They taught me how to thrive by faith, not by sight.

I'm extremely grateful for everything I endured in life. And I mean everything—the good and the bad. On the good side, I earned an associate degree in the administration of justice, a bachelor's degree in criminal justice, and a juris doctorate in law. I recently transitioned from a thirty-year public service career to pursue work with community-based agencies and institutions dedicated to serving the foster care community. Giving back is my way of extending the legacy of God's grace and kingdom by living a life of service, purpose, and leadership. This is the inheritance that matters most and the one that I will leave to my two children and my adorable grandson.

On the bad side, I'm still learning how to lean into what I know to be true by God's grace and spirit, rather than following the impulse to go it alone, as I did during my youth. All I've accomplished and all I have yet to do in serving others flows from the belief that with the right foundation anchored by Christ, we can help foster children who thrive in all areas of life. And even when we're not thriving, we're doing more than surviving because of our hope and connection to the creator, giver, and sustainer of life.

Mandy's Story

From the beginning of time, there was a plan. You and I were created as a special part of that plan. Our part is our ever-unfolding story He is writing through our lives. We were put here to love Jesus, show our scars, and tell our story.

To tell you my story *is to tell of Him!* Oftentimes God uses the circumstances of our lives to form the framework for the message He desires to speak in and through us.

My story begins in a small town in Georgia. I was born into a home suffering from the effects of poverty, alcoholism, and drug addiction thus resulting in severe neglect and abuse of every form. Our home was not a portrait of hope and happiness. My mother's first marriage ended abruptly after she was given an ultimatum—end her pregnancy with me or my father would leave her. She chose life for me and soon found herself a poor, single mother of three. Her second marriage was not derived of love but one driven by desperation to care for her children.

My stepfather's vices created horrific conditions and would eventually lead to destruction. Every day was a desperate struggle to survive. On any given day my mother could be seen knocking at the back door of neighbors begging or bartering for food or perhaps seeking a safe haven for just a little while. As my two brothers and I grew, so did the challenges she faced. Eventually the daily struggle to survive, provide, and protect would take its toll on my mother.

One particular day started out like any other day . . . in our home, filled with rage and violence. But on this particular day, my mother became far too weary and no longer had the stamina or strength to survive. On this day, the violence would take her life . . . right before my very eyes.

It was more than a day before my neighbors suspected something was wrong and made the call. When the authorities arrived, they found my mother's body—beaten, strangled, and lying on the edge of the bed. In the corner they found an abandoned, battered little girl, shivering . . . fearful to be touched but desperate to be loved. The appropriate calls were made. When no one came forward to claim me, I became a ward of the state and officially entered the foster care system.

Though I had few belongings, much baggage would accompany me.

For scars and wounds are not checked at the gate but are carry-on baggage. Where I went . . . so did the impact and trauma of all I had suffered and experienced.

Despite the trauma endured before placement, and the continued disruption caused by placement, a foster child is expected to arrive on the doorstep of their new home with a thank-you note . . . as if the impact and trauma of life never occurred and was not impressed deeply into the heart, mind, and very being of that child. Far too often these children are expected to walk into our schools and churches under the same false pretenses.

Many years passed as I continued in the foster care system. I found myself once again relocated and assigned a new social worker, Ms. B. She read the case file and familiarized herself with my history. She knew the emotional challenges I faced.

After quite some time in this new Christ-following home she began to notice significant progress and evidence indicating healing in my life. Trust was surfacing. Real hope seemed to be on the horizon. Something was quite different about this family and their approach with me. I had endured other foster families that unfortunately fed my emotional challenges and deepened my wounds. But this family loved and kept loving, unconditionally, no matter what. They were able to see beyond my behaviors, pouring into who they believed I could be and who God created me to become—for His plan—His purpose. They needed, and sought every possible form of support, resource, and willing person to wrap around me and our family—each person necessary and playing a different role in our "village."

Ms. B became concerned when discussions arose to move me for the purpose of permanency. At this time federal laws prohibited a fostering family to adopt a foster child placed in their temporary care. She knew the law, but in her heart she was painfully aware that another move, yet another disruption and heartbreak, could be detrimental. With a determined spirit, my parents, along with Ms. B, tenaciously fought for me every step of the way—upstream and against conventional thinking. They never gave up because they knew the truth of Jeremiah 29:11, and they knew hope and healing was on the horizon.

Because of their fight, I was eventually adopted. I grew in the love and nurturing of my new forever family, blessed to be faithfully wrapped around by my local church family. Through their yes, I learned of the greatest love, the love of my Heavenly Father, and would later be adopted spiritually into God's family as well. I remember my first Christmas after the adoption was completed. I remember bolting down the stairs, running to the tree, and tearing through the presents. Not in search of the largest gift but for the present with the tag that read, "To: Mandy, From: Mom & Dad." You see I could have a Santa any day of the year, but I finally had a mom and dad of my very own.

I experienced healing through the nurturing love and faithful prayers of my parents as they extended tangible grace, imitating His love as defender, provider, and protector. Because they tenaciously fought and never gave up, because they accepted the grand invitation set before them, I stand today: grace on display. God has taken the mess of my life and turned it into a powerful message of hope. *Messy* does not mean *mistake!* It's worth the fight!

Our story isn't over yet. He takes the broken pieces of our lives and is writing a new story of redemption. He wastes nothing. He will redeem our suffering. For me, what could have been a story of ultimate destruction and brokenness is now abundant blessings. Along the way, God invites others to be a part of the journey, to travel together, and witness the process of my redemption. Some (like my parents, my local church, and Ms. B) accepted the challenge. They are my champions! Their passion, tenacity, and due diligence played a significant role in my life, my healing, and the lives of many to come. Their resounding, fear-filled, faithful yes created ripples of hope for generations to come.

Today, our family has been called to an incredible journey. God has afforded me the privilege of now being the blessed mother of seventeen beautiful children. Equipped by my own experiences and now investing in the lives of our children, I am allowing God to use my scars as agents of healing in the lives of others at home and around the world. I am honored to stand as a voice for youth in foster care everywhere. In addition to wife and mom, I am an international keynote speaker, advocate, writer, and trauma informed instructor. My husband and I founded Safe Harbor Orphan Care Ministries as a means to share our story, advocate, and equip families, churches, and communities to adopt, foster, and offer support. My story of redemption continues on all because a family said yes to God's request. You never knew what lies on the other side of your yes. Because a family, one social worker, and an incredible church family determined to tenaciously fight for one. And that it was worth the fight. I am evidence that God is always writing a bigger and better story than we can *ever* imagine!

NOTES

1 John DeGarmo, "Modern Day Slavery Does Exist in America: How Our Children Are Victims Today," *HuffPost*, March 17, 2017, https://www.huffington post.com/entry/modern-day-slavery-does-exist-in-america-how-our-children _us_58ac3afae4b029c1d1f88ead.

2 John DeGarmo, "The Shocking Truth of Child Sex Trafficking," *HuffPost*, November 18, 2016, https://www.huffingtonpost.com/entry/the-shocking-truth -of-child-sex-trafficking_us_582de812e4b0eaa5f14d417d.

3 John DeGarmo, "How Today's Children Are Victims of Cyberbullying," Kids in the House, March 3, 2016, https://www.kidsinthehouse.com/blogs/dr -john-degarmo/how-todays-children-are-victims-of-cyberbullying.

4 John DeGarmo, "America's Opioid Crisis: How Children Are Casualties," *HuffPost*, March 17, 2017, https://www.huffingtonpost.com/entry/americas -opioid-crisis-how-children-are-casualties_us_58b44ecfe4b0658fc20f9828.

5 John DeGarmo, "How the Heroin Crisis Is Straining Foster Care," *HuffPost*, April 11, 2017, https://www.huffingtonpost.com/entry/how-the-heroin-crisis -is-straining-foster-care_us_58ed0740e4b0ea028d568d3c.

6 John DeGarmo, "Why America's Babies Are Suffering: Opioid Addictions Placing More Babies in Foster Care," *HuffPost*, April 20, 2017, https://www .huffingtonpost.com/entry/why-americas-babies-are-suffering-opioid -addictions_us_58f8b468e4b0b6ca13416171.

7 John DeGarmo, "Visitations and Foster Children," FosterCare Institute, August 11, 2013, https://www.drjohndegarmofostercare.com/blog/visitations-and-foster -children.

8 John Degarmo, "A Forever Family: Adoption from Foster Care," *Medium*, March 16, 2015, https://medium.com/@drjohndegarmo/a-forever-family-adoption-from-foster-care-27d04d8e3f43.

9 John DeGarmo, "Foster Care and the Need for Clothing," *Foster Focus*, Vol. 2, Iss. 9, https://www.fosterfocusmag.com/articles/foster-care-need-clothing.

10 John Degarmo, "Foster Care and the Need for Clothing," *Foster Focus*, Vol. 2, Iss. 9, https://www.fosterfocusmag.com/articles/foster-care-need-clothing.

11 John DeGarmo, "Are You the Reason Our Children Are Failing in School?" *HuffPost*, August 24, 2015, https://www.huffingtonpost.com/dr-john-degarmo/the-reason-children-in-school_b_7987564.html.

12 John DeGarmo, "The Tragedy of Turning Eighteen: Aging Out of Foster Care," Kids in the House, May 24, 2016, https://www.kidsinthehouse.com/blogs/dr-john-degarmo/the-tragedy-of-turning-18-aging-out-of-foster-care.

SCRIPTURE VERSES
FOR FOSTER PARENTS

GOD'S CALL TO CARE FOR CHILDREN

FOR I WAS HUNGRY AND YOU GAVE ME SOMETHING TO EAT,
I WAS THIRSTY AND YOU GAVE ME SOMETHING TO DRINK,
I WAS A STRANGER AND YOU INVITED ME IN, I NEEDED CLOTHES
AND YOU CLOTHED ME, I WAS SICK AND YOU LOOKED AFTER ME,
I WAS IN PRISON AND YOU CAME TO VISIT ME.
—MATTHEW 25:35–36

LEARN TO DO RIGHT; SEEK JUSTICE. DEFEND THE OPPRESSED.
TAKE UP THE CAUSE OF THE FATHERLESS;
PLEAD THE CASE OF THE WIDOW.
—ISAIAH 1:17–18

HE TOOK A LITTLE CHILD WHOM HE PLACED AMONG THEM.
TAKING THE CHILD IN HIS ARMS, HE SAID TO THEM,
"WHOEVER WELCOMES ONE OF THESE LITTLE CHILDREN
IN MY NAME WELCOMES ME; AND WHOEVER WELCOMES ME
DOES NOT WELCOME ME BUT THE ONE WHO SENT ME."
—MARK 9:36–37

He has shown you, O mortal, what is good. And what does the Lord require of you? To act justly and to love mercy and to walk humbly with your God.
—Micah 6:8

Whoever welcomes one such child in my name welcomes me. If anyone causes one of these little ones—those who believe in me—to stumble, it would be better for them to have a large millstone hung around their neck and to be drowned in the depths of the sea.
—Matthew 18:5–6

Then the people brought little children to Jesus for him to place his hands on them and pray for them. But the disciples rebuked them. Jesus said, "Let the little children come to me, and do not hinder them, for the kingdom of heaven belongs to such as these." When he placed his hands on them, he went away from there.
—Matthew 19:13–15

Religion that God our Father accepts as pure and faultless is this: to look after orphans and widows in their distress and to keep oneself from being polluted by the world.
—James 1:27

Defend the weak and the fatherless; uphold the cause of the poor and the oppressed. Rescue the weak and the needy; deliver them from the hand of the wicked.
—Psalm 82:3–4

God's Words about Using Our Talents

For we are God's handiwork, created in Christ Jesus to do good works, which God prepared in advance for us to do.
—Ephesians 2:10

Every good and perfect gift is from above, coming down from the Father of the heavenly lights, who does not change like shifting shadows.
—James 1:17

Do you see someone skilled in their work?
They will serve before kings; they will not
serve before officials of low rank.
—Proverbs 22:29

Each of you should use whatever gift you have
received to serve others, as faithful stewards
of God's grace in its various forms. If anyone speaks,
they should do so as one who speaks the very words of
God. If anyone serves, they should do so with the strength
God provides, so that in all things God may be praised
through Jesus Christ. To him be the glory and the power
for ever and ever. Amen.
—1 Peter 4:10–11

Now about the gifts of the Spirit, brothers and sisters,
I do not want you to be uninformed. You know that when
you were pagans, somehow or other you were influenced
and led astray to mute idols. Therefore I want you to
know that no one who is speaking by the Spirit of God says,
"Jesus be cursed," and no one can say, "Jesus is Lord,"
except by the Holy Spirit. There are different kinds of
gifts, but the same Spirit distributes them. *There
are different kinds of service, but the same Lord. There are
different kinds of working, but in all of them and in everyone
it is the same God at work.* Now to each one the
manifestation of the Spirit is given for the common good.
To one there is given through the Spirit a message of
wisdom, to another a message of knowledge by means of
the same Spirit, to another faith by the same Spirit, to
another gifts of healing by that one Spirit, to another
miraculous powers, to another prophecy, to another
distinguishing between spirits, to another speaking in
different kinds of tongues, and to still another the
interpretation of tongues. All these are the work of one
and the same Spirit, and he distributes them to each one,
just as he determines.
—1 Corinthians 12:1–11 (emphasis added)

GOD'S WORD ABOUT ADOPTION

GOD DECIDED IN ADVANCE TO ADOPT US INTO HIS OWN FAMILY BY BRINGING US TO HIMSELF THROUGH JESUS CHRIST. THIS IS WHAT HE WANTED TO DO, AND IT GAVE HIM GREAT PLEASURE.
—EPHESIANS 1:5 NLT

RELIGION THAT GOD OUR FATHER ACCEPTS AS PURE
AND FAULTLESS IS THIS: TO LOOK AFTER ORPHANS
AND WIDOWS IN THEIR DISTRESS AND TO KEEP ONESELF
FROM BEING POLLUTED BY THE WORLD.
—JAMES 1:27

DEFEND THE WEAK AND THE FATHERLESS;
UPHOLD THE CAUSE OF THE POOR AND THE OPPRESSED.
—PSALM 82:3

HE DEFENDS THE CAUSE OF THE FATHERLESS
AND THE WIDOW, AND LOVES THE FOREIGNER RESIDING
AMONG YOU, GIVING THEM FOOD AND CLOTHING.
—DEUTERONOMY 10:18

GOD'S WORD ABOUT CLOTHING THE LEAST OF THESE

IS IT NOT TO SHARE YOUR FOOD WITH THE HUNGRY
AND TO PROVIDE THE POOR WANDERER WITH SHELTER—WHEN YOU
SEE THE NAKED, TO CLOTHE THEM, AND NOT TO TURN AWAY FROM
YOUR OWN FLESH AND BLOOD?
—ISAIAH 58:7

JOHN ANSWERED, "ANYONE WHO HAS TWO SHIRTS
SHOULD SHARE WITH THE ONE WHO HAS NONE,
AND ANYONE WHO HAS FOOD SHOULD DO THE SAME."
—LUKE 3:11

I NEEDED CLOTHES AND YOU CLOTHED ME, I WAS SICK
AND YOU LOOKED AFTER ME, I WAS IN PRISON
AND YOU CAME TO VISIT ME.
—MATTHEW 25:36

BUT [HE] GIVES HIS FOOD TO THE HUNGRY
AND PROVIDES CLOTHING FOR THE NAKED.
—EZEKIEL 18:16

GOD'S WORD ABOUT THE POWER OF PRAYER

ASK AND IT WILL BE GIVEN TO YOU; SEEK AND YOU WILL FIND;
KNOCK AND THE DOOR WILL BE OPENED TO YOU.
—MATTHEW 7:7

IF YOU BELIEVE, YOU WILL RECEIVE
WHATEVER YOU ASK FOR IN PRAYER.
—MATTHEW 21:22

THEREFORE I TELL YOU, WHATEVER YOU ASK IN PRAYER,
BELIEVE THAT YOU HAVE RECEIVED IT, AND IT WILL BE YOURS.
—MARK 11:24

AND I WILL DO WHATEVER YOU ASK IN MY NAME, SO THAT THE
FATHER MAY BE GLORIFIED IN THE SON. YOU MAY ASK ME FOR
ANYTHING IN MY NAME, AND I WILL DO IT.
—JOHN 14:13–14

IS ANYONE AMONG YOU SICK? LET THEM CALL THE ELDERS OF THE
CHURCH TO PRAY OVER THEM AND ANOINT THEM WITH OIL IN THE
NAME OF THE LORD. AND THE PRAYER OFFERED IN FAITH WILL
MAKE THE SICK PERSON WELL; THE LORD WILL RAISE THEM UP.
IF THEY HAVE SINNED, THEY WILL BE FORGIVEN. THEREFORE
CONFESS YOUR SINS TO EACH OTHER AND PRAY FOR EACH OTHER
SO THAT YOU MAY BE HEALED. THE PRAYER OF A RIGHTEOUS
PERSON IS POWERFUL AND EFFECTIVE.
—JAMES 5:14–16

DO NOT BE ANXIOUS ABOUT ANYTHING, BUT IN EVERY SITUATION,
BY PRAYER AND PETITION, WITH THANKSGIVING, PRESENT YOUR
REQUESTS TO GOD. AND THE PEACE OF GOD, WHICH TRANSCENDS
ALL UNDERSTANDING, WILL GUARD YOUR HEARTS
AND YOUR MINDS IN CHRIST JESUS.
—PHILIPPIANS 4:6–7

DEVOTE YOURSELVES TO PRAYER, BEING WATCHFUL AND THANKFUL.
—COLOSSIANS 4:2

THEREFORE I TELL YOU, WHATEVER YOU ASK FOR IN PRAYER,
BELIEVE THAT YOU HAVE RECEIVED IT, AND IT WILL BE YOURS.
—MARK 11:24

FOR WHERE TWO OR THREE GATHER IN MY NAME,
THERE AM I WITH THEM.
—MATTHEW 18:20

Foster Care Contact Information By State

ALABAMA
DEPARTMENT OF
HUMAN RESOURCES
Center for Communications
GORDON PERSONS BUILDING
SUITE 2104
50 NORTH RIPLEY STREET
MONTGOMERY, AL 36130
PHONE: 334-242-1310

WEBSITE:
http://dhr.alabama.gov
/services/Foster_Care/FC_
Children_Teens.aspx

ALASKA
DEPARTMENT OF HEALTH
AND SOCIAL SERVICES
350 MAIN STREET, ROOM 404
PO BOX 110601
JUNEAU, AK 99811-0601
PHONE: 907-465-3030

WEBSITE:
http://hss.state.ak.us/ocs
/fostercare/default.htm

ARKANSAS
DEPARTMENT OF
HUMAN SERVICES
Division of Children and Family Services
PO Box 1437, Slot S-560
Little Rock, AR 72203-1437
Phone: 501-682-8770

Website:
www.fosterarkansas.org

ARIZONA
DEPARTMENT OF
CHILD SAFETY
PO Box 6123 Site Code 940A
Phoenix, AZ 85005-6123
Phone: 1-877-543-7633

Website: www.des.az.gov

CALIFORNIA
DEPARTMENT OF
SOCIAL SERVICES
744 P Street
Sacramento, CA 95814
Phone: 916-657-2614

Website:
www.cdss.ca.gov

COLORADO
DEPARTMENT OF
HUMAN SERVICES
1575 Sherman Street, 2nd Floor
Denver, CO 80203
Phone: 1-800-799-5876

Website:
www.co4kids.org

CONNECTICUT
STATE DEPARTMENT
OF CHILDREN AND FAMILIES
505 Hudson Street
Hartford, CT 06106
Phone: 860-550-6300

Website:
www.portal.ct.gov/dcf

DELAWARE
DEPARTMENT OF
SERVICES
for Children, Youth, and their Families
1825 Faulkland Road
Wilmington, DE 19805
Phone: 302-633-2657

Website:
http://kids.delaware.gov/fs
/fostercare.shtml

DISTRICT OF COLUMBIA
CHILD AND FAMILY SERVICES AGENCY
200 I Street, SE
Washington, DC 20003
Phone: 202-442-6100

Website: www.cfsa.dc.gov

FLORIDA
DEPARTMENT OF CHILDREN AND FAMILIES
1317 Winewood Blvd.
Building 1, Room 202
Tallahassee, FL 32399-0700
Phone: 850-487-1111

Website: www.myflfamilies.com

GEORGIA
DIVISION OF FAMILY AND CHILDREN SERVICES
2 Peachtree Street, NW
Suite 18-486
Atlanta, GA 30303
Phone: 404-651-9361

Website:
http://dfcs.dhs.georgia.gov
/portal/site/DHS-DFCS/

HAWAII
DEPARTMENT OF HUMAN SERVICES
1390 Miller Street
Room 209
Honolulu, HI 96813
Phone: 808-586-5679

Website:
www.humanservices.hawaii.gov

IDAHO
DEPARTMENT OF HEALTH AND WELFARE
PO Box 83720
Boise, ID 83720-0036
Phone: 800-926-2588

Website:
http://www.healthandwelfare
.idaho.gov/Children
/AdoptionFosterCareHome
/tabid/75/Default.aspx

ILLINOIS
DEPARTMENT OF CHILDREN AND FAMILY SERVICES
406 East Monroe Street
Springfield, IL 62701
Phone: 1-800-572-2390

Website:
www.state.il.us/dcfs/foster
/index.shtml

INDIANA
DEPARTMENT OF
CHILD SERVICES
302 West Washington Street
Room E306
Indianapolis, IN 46204
Phone: 1-888-631-9510

Website:
www.in.gov/dcs/index.htm

IOWA
DEPARTMENT OF
HUMAN SERVICES
1305 E. Walnut St.
Des Moines, IA 50319-0114
Phone: 515-281-5521

Website:
www.dhs.iowa.gov

KANSAS
DEPARTMENT FOR
CHILDREN AND FAMILIES
555 S. Kansas Avenue
Topeka, KS 66603
Phone: 785-296-3271

Website:
www.srs.ks.gov/agency/Pages
/AgencyInformation.aspx

KENTUCKY
CABINET FOR HEALTH
AND FAMILY SERVICES
275 E. Main St.
Frankfort, KY 40621
Phone: 1-800-372-2973

Website:
http://chfs.ky.gov/

LOUISIANA
DEPARTMENT OF
CHILDREN AND FAMILY
SERVICES
627 N. 4th St.
Baton Rouge, LA 70802
Phone: 888-524-3578

Website:
www.dss.state.la.us

MAINE
OFFICE OF CHILD
AND FAMILY SERVICES
2 Anthony Avenue
Augusta, ME 04333-0011
Phone: 207-624-7900

Website:
www.maine.gov/dhhs/ocfs

MARYLAND
DEPARTMENT OF
HUMAN SERVICES
311 West Saratoga St.
Baltimore, MD 21201
Phone: 1-800-332-6347

Website:
www.dhr.maryland.gov
/foster-care

MASSACHUSETTS
DEPARTMENT OF
CHILDREN AND FAMILIES
600 Washington St.
6th Floor
Boston, MA 02111
Phone: 617-748-2000

Website:
www.mass.gov/eohhs/gov
/departments/dcf

MICHIGAN
DEPARTMENT OF
HUMAN SERVICES
235 S. Grand Ave.
PO Box 30037
Lansing, Michigan 48909
Phone: 1-866-540-0008

Website:
www.michigan.gov/mdhhs
/0,5885,7-339-73971_7117—,00.html

MINNESOTA
DEPARTMENT OF
HUMAN SERVICES
PO Box 64244
St. Paul, MN 55164-0244
Phone: 651-431-3830

Website:
http://mn.gov/dhs

MISSOURI
DEPARTMENT OF
SOCIAL SERVICES
Broadway State Office Building
P.O. Box 1527
Jefferson City, MO 65102-1527
Telephone: 573-751-4815

Website: www.dss.mo.gov/cd
/foster-care

MISSISSIPPI
DEPARTMENT OF
CHILD PROTECTION
SERVICES
660 North St. #200
Jackson, MS 39202
Phone: 601-359-4785

Website:
www.mdcps.ms.gov

NEBRASKA
DIVISION OF CHILDREN
AND FAMILY SERVICES
PO Box 95026
Lincoln, NE 68509-5044
Phone: 402-471-9272

Website:
http://dhhs.ne.gov/children
_family_services/Pages/foc
_focindex.aspx

NEVADA
DIVISION OF CHILD AND
FAMILY SERVICES
4126 Technology Way, 3rd
Floor
Carson City, NV 89706
Phone: 775-684-4400

Website:
www.dcfs.state.nv.us

NEW HAMPSHIRE
DEPARTMENT OF HEALTH
AND HUMAN SERVICES
129 Pleasant St.
Concord, NH 03301-3852
Phone: (603) 271-4711

Website:
www.dhhs.nh.gov/dcyf/index.htm

NEW JERSEY
DEPARTMENT OF
CHILDREN AND FAMILIES
PO Box 729
Trenton, NJ 08625-0729
Phone: 1-855-463-6323

Website:
www.state.nj.us/dcf/index.shtml

NEW MEXICO
CHILDREN, YOUTH, AND
FAMILIES DEPARTMENT
PO Drawer 5160
Santé Fe, NM 87502-5160
Phone: 800-432-2075

Website:
www.cyfd.org

NEW YORK
OFFICE OF CHILDREN
AND FAMILY SERVICES
52 Washington St.
Rensselaer, NY 12144-2834
Phone: 800-345-5437

Website:
www.ocfs.ny.gov/main
/fostercare

NORTH CAROLINA
DEPARTMENT OF HEALTH
AND HUMAN SERVICES
2001 MAIL SERVICE CENTER
RALEIGH, NC 27699-2001
PHONE: 1-877-625-4371

WEBSITE:
https://www.ncdhhs.gov
/assistance/state-guardianship
/foster-care

NORTH DAKOTA
DEPARTMENT OF CHILDREN
AND FAMILY SERVICES
600 E. BOULEVARD AVE., DEPT. 325
BISMARCK, ND 58505
PHONE: 701-328-2316

WEBSITE:
www.nd.gov/dhs/services
/childfamily/fostercare

OHIO
DEPARTMENT OF JOBS
AND FAMILY SERVICES
4200 E. FIFTH AVENUE, 2ND FLOOR
COLUMBUS, OH 43219
PHONE: 614-466-1213

WEBSITE:
www.jfs.ohio.gov/ocomm_
root/0002OurServices.stm

OKLAHOMA
DEPARTMENT OF
HUMAN SERVICES
5905 N. CLASSEN CT. STE 401
OKLAHOMA CITY, OK 73118-5940
PHONE: 1-800-376-9729

WEBSITE:
www.okdhs.org/services/foster
/Pages/FosterCareHome.aspx

OREGON
DEPARTMENT OF
HUMAN SERVICES
500 SUMMER ST. NE E-15
SALEM, OR 97301
PHONE: 1-800-331-0503

WEBSITE:
www.oregon.gov/DHS/children

PENNSYLVANIA
DEPARTMENT OF
HUMAN SERVICES
PO BOX 2675
HARRISBURG, PA 17105-2675
PHONE: 800-692-7462

WEBSITE:
www.dhs.pa.gov/citizens
/childwelfareservices
/fostercareinpennsylvania

RHODE ISLAND
DEPARTMENT OF
CHILDREN, YOUTH,
AND FAMILIES
101 FRIENDSHIP STREET
PROVIDENCE, RI 02903-3716
PHONE: 401-528-3500

WEBSITE:
www.dcyf.ri.gov/foster/index.php

SOUTH CAROLINA
DEPARTMENT FOR
CHILDREN AND FAMILIES
PO BOX 1520
COLUMBIA, SC 29202-1520
PHONE: 803-898-7601

WEBSITE:
www.dss.sc.gov/foster-care

SOUTH DAKOTA
DEPARTMENT OF
SOCIAL SERVICES
700 GOVERNORS DRIVE
PIERRE, SD 57501
PHONE: 605-773- 3227

WEBSITE:
www.dss.sd.gov/childprotection
/fostercare/parent.aspx

TENNESSEE
DEPARTMENT OF
CHILDREN'S SERVICES
UBS TOWER, 10TH FLOOR
315 DEADERICK STREET
NASHVILLE, TN 37243
PHONE: 615-741-9701

WEBSITE:
www.tn.gov/dcs/program-areas
/fca.html

TEXAS
DEPARTMENT OF
FAMILY AND
PROTECTIVE SERVICES
701 W. 51ST ST
AUSTIN, TX 78751
PHONE: 1-800-233-3405

WEBSITE:
www.dfps.state.tx.us

UTAH
DEPARTMENT OF CHILD
AND FAMILY SERVICES
195 NORTH 1950 WEST
SALT LAKE CITY, UT 84116
PHONE: 801-994-5205

WEBSITE:
http://dcfs.utah.gov/services
/foster-care

VERMONT
DEPARTMENT FOR
CHILDREN AND FAMILIES
280 STATE DRIVE
WATERBURY, VT 05671-1030
PHONE: 800-649-2642

WEBSITE:
www.dcf.vermont.gov/foster

VIRGINIA
DEPARTMENT OF
SOCIAL SERVICES
801 E. MAIN STREET
RICHMOND, VA 23219
PHONE: 800-468-8894

WEBSITE:
www.dss.virginia.gov/family/fc
/index.cgi

WASHINGTON
STATE DEPARTMENT
OF CHILDREN, YOUTH,
AND FAMILIES
PO BOX 45130
OLYMPIA, WA 98504-5130
PHONE: 1-888-543-7414

WEBSITE:
www.dshs.wa.gov/ca/general
/index.asp

WEST VIRGINIA
BUREAU FOR CHILDREN
AND FAMILIES
350 CAPITOL STREET, ROOM 691
CHARLESTON, WEST VIRGINIA 25301
PHONE: 866-225-5698

WEBSITE:
www.dhhr.wv.gov/bcf
/Providers/Pages/Adoption.aspx

WISCONSIN
DEPARTMENT OF
CHILDREN AND FAMILIES
201 E. WASHINGTON AVE.
SECOND FLOOR
P.O. BOX 8916
MADISON, WI 53708-8916
PHONE: 800-947-8074

WEBSITE:
www.dcf.wisconsin.gov
/fostercare/parent

WYOMING
DEPARTMENT OF
FAMILY SERVICES
2300 CAPITOL AVENUE
THIRD FLOOR
CHEYENNE, WY 82002
PHONE: 1-800-457-3659

WEBSITE:
http://dfsweb.wyo.gov/social
-services/foster-care

Organizations Helping Children in Foster Care

AGAPE

4555 Trousdale Drive
Nashville, Tennessee 37204
WWW.AGAPENASHVILLE.ORG

AMARIS MINISTRIES

585 W. Orange Avenue, Suite 1
El Centro, CA 92243
WWW.AMARISMINISTRIES.COM

AMG INTERNATIONAL

6815 Shallowford Road
Chattanooga, TN 37421
WWW.AMGINTERNATIONAL.ORG

ARROW CHILD AND FAMILY MINISTRIES
2929 FM 2920 Rd.
Spring, Texas 77388
WWW.ARROW.ORG

BECCA'S CLOSET
151 North Nob Hill Road, Suite 280
Plantation, FL 33324
WWW.BECCASCLOSET.ORG

BETHANY CHRISTIAN SERVICES
901 Eastern Ave. NE
Grand Rapids, MI 49503
WWW.BETHANY.ORG

CHRISTIAN FAMILY CARE
3603 North 7th Ave.
Phoenix, AZ 85013
WWW.CFCARE.ORG

DAVE THOMAS FOUNDATION FOR ADOPTION
716 Mt. Airyshire Blvd., Suite 100
Columbus, OH 43235
WWW.DAVETHOMASFOUNDATION.ORG

FOCUS ON YOUTH
8904 Brookside Ave.
West Chester, OH 45069
WWW.FOCUSONYOUTH.COM

FOCUS ON THE FAMILY
8605 Explorer Drive
Colorado Springs, CO 80920-1051
WWW.FOCUSONTHEFAMILY.COM

FOSTER CARE CLOSET

643 S25th Street, Suite 8
Lincoln, NE 68510
WWW.FOSTERCARECLOSET.ORG

FOSTER CLOSET

8307 Beach Blvd.
Jacksonville, FL 32216
WWW.FOSTERCLOSET.ORG

HANDS OF HOPE ADOPTION AND ORPHAN CARE MINISTRY

14350 Mundy Drive, Suite 800 #119
Noblesville, IN 46060
WWW.HANDSOFHOPEIN.ORG

KIDS IN A NEW GROOVE

3737 Executive Center Drive #154
Austin, TX 78731
WWW.KIDSINANEWGROOVE.ORG

LIFELINE CHILDREN'S SERVICE

100 Missionary Ridge
Birmingham, AL 35242
WWW.LIFELINECHILD.ORG

MAKE A CHANGE INC.

PO Box 1141
Gardner, MA 01440
WWW.MAKEACHANGEINC.ORG

OLIVE CREST

2130 E. 4th St., Suite 200
Santa Ana, CA 92705
WWW.OLIVECREST.ORG

NATIONAL COUNCIL FOR ADOPTION

225 N. Washington Street
Alexandria, VA 22314
WWW.ADOPTIONCOUNCIL.ORG

NATIONAL FOSTER PARENT ASSOCIATION

1102 Prairie Ridge Trail
Pflugerville, TX 78660
WWW.NFPAONLINE.ORG

ONEHOPE27

Milwaukee, WI
WWW.ONEHOPE27.ORG

THE ORANGE DUFFEL BAG INITIATIVE

1801 Peachtree St. NE, Suite 300
Atlanta, GA 30309
WWW.THEODBI.ORG

PROJECT 1.27

2220 S Chambers Road
Aurora, CO 80014
WWW.PROJECT127.COM

PROMISE 686

4729 Peachtree Industrial Blvd., Suite 100
Berkeley Lake, GA 30092
WWW.PROMISE686.ORG

ROYAL FAMILY KIDS

3000 W. MacArthur Blvd., Suite 412
Santa Ana, CA 92704
WWW.RFK.ORG

TAPESTRY FAMILY SERVICES

290 East Gobbi St.
Ukiah, CA 95482
WWW.TAPESTRYFS.ORG

TOGETHER WE RISE

580 W Lambert Rd., #A,
Brea, CA 92821
WWW.TOGETHERWERISE.ORG

TRAVELING TUTUS INC.

795 E. Lakeshore Blvd.
Kissimmee, FL 34744
WWW.TRAVELINGTUTUS.ORG

THE UNITED METHODIST CHILDREN'S HOME

1967 Lakeside Parkway, Suite 400
Tucker, GA 30084
WWW.UMCHILDRENSHOME.ORG

WINSHAPE

PO Box 490007
Mt. Berry, GA 30149
WWW.WINSHAPE.ORG

If you enjoyed this book, will you consider sharing the message with others?

Let us know your thoughts at info@newhopepublishers.com.
You can also let the author know by visiting or sharing a photo of
the cover on our social media pages or leaving a review at a retailer's site.
All of it helps us get the message out!

Twitter.com/NewHopeBooks

Facebook.com/NewHopePublishers

Instagram.com/NewHopePublishers

———————

New Hope® Publishers is an imprint of Iron Stream Media,
which derives its name from Proverbs 27:17,
"As iron sharpens iron, so one person sharpens another."

This sharpening describes the process of discipleship, one to another. With
this in mind, Iron Stream Media provides a variety of solutions for churches,
missionaries, and nonprofits ranging from in-depth Bible study curriculum
and Christian book publishing to custom publishing and consultative
services. Through the popular Life Bible Study and Student Life Bible Study
brands, ISM provides web-based full-year and short-term Bible study teaching
plans as well as printed devotionals, Bibles, and discipleship curriculum.

For more information on ISM and New Hope Publishers, please visit

IronStreamMedia.com

NewHopePublishers.com

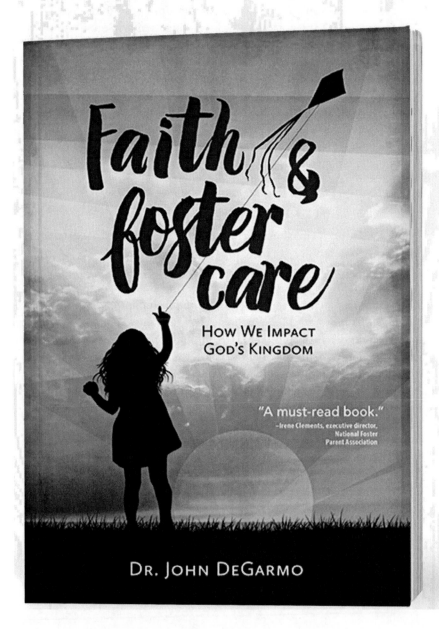

OTHER
Adoption
Resources

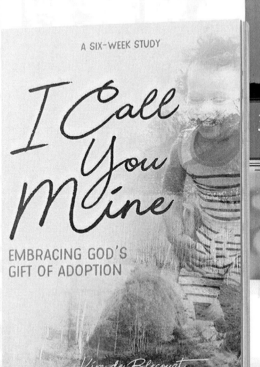

A SIX-WEEK STUDY

I Call You Mine

EMBRACING GOD'S
GIFT OF ADOPTION

Kim de Blecourt

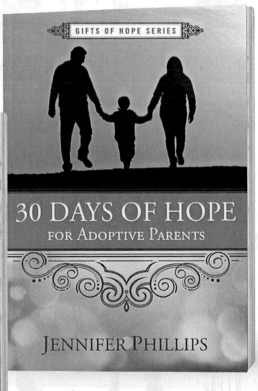

GIFTS OF HOPE SERIES

30 DAYS OF HOPE
FOR ADOPTIVE PARENTS

JENNIFER PHILLIPS

We hope you found the information in *The Church and Foster Care: God's Call to a Growing Epidemic* beneficial. Here's an excerpt from Dr. DeGarmo's book, *Faith and Foster Care: How We Impact God's Kingdom,* also from New Hope Publishers.

CALLED TO FOSTER

*T*he urgency in my wife's voice was unmistakable. "John!" she called out to me, a second time. In my 14 years of marriage to my Australian bride, I had never heard such insistence in Kelly's voice, and I found it a little troubling.

"Coming," I said back to her. I was in the kitchen preparing dinner for the six children in our home while holding our newest foster daughter in my arms, who was screaming and using her small and fragile lungs to the utmost. The four-month-old infant, named Melinda, had done nothing but scream since she first arrived the day before, along with her four-year-old brother, Donnie. The tiny, underweight child was born addicted to the drug meth, our first experience with a meth-addicted child. My previous research had taught me that babies born to mothers addicted to meth generally suffer from a number of possible symptoms. Furthermore, I also found that these babies often suffer from brain damage, respiratory problems, neurological damage, organ damage, and general poor health. Melinda's nonstop screaming was probably due to the fact that the four month old was easily agitated, due to emotional problems, and sadly would most likely be for the rest of her life. Easily agitated. That would explain why she screamed, kicked, and fussed every waking moment. My heart had immediately broken when I found that this tiny little baby, innocent in all ways, suffered due to her biological mother's need to take the illegal drug. Handing her over to my 11-year-old daughter, I rushed into the bathroom, hoping to discover the cause of Kelly's distress.

When I arrived in our bathroom, I found my wife sitting next to the bathtub with tears streaming down her face. "What's wrong?" I promptly asked. During our years of marriage, and even before then during our time in the international performing group Up With People, where I first met Kelly as we traveled across the globe singing and dancing in front of thousands live and millions more on television, I had never seen her speechless before. Visibly upset, she had no words for me. Again I asked her, "What's wrong?"

As she tried to gather herself, Kelly pointed to the child's head, whereupon she feebly said between sobs, "Look."

Peering down at the four year old's blond hair, I was unable to see the cause of her concern. "I don't see anything," I replied.

Parting back Donnie's hair, my wife then repeated her earnest request: "*Look.*"

Looking down, I saw several tiny black circular marks on our foster son's head, marks I had not seen before, nor was certain of what they might represent. At first glance, they looked to be round burn marks, some fresh in appearance. "What are they?" I asked.

"Cigarette burns," my wife simply replied, wiping tears from her face. At this, I gasped in horror as the realization of what was before my eyes began to sink in. "Donnie, tell Mr. John how you got that booboo," she asked the child.

"That's where my mommy put her cigarettes when I get into trouble." He said it so matter of factly, as if it was a common occurrence, as if it was common practice for all adults when punishing their child.

Startled, I then asked, "Donnie, did your mommy put cigarettes anywhere else?" God, please no, I thought to myself.

"In here," the child said, opening his mouth wide and pointing to his tongue.

Bending over the tub, Kelly peered into Donnie's mouth. Shaking her head to indicate that there were some more burn spots on his tongue as well as the roof of his mouth, my wife quietly whispered to me, "She was probably trying to hide the evidence." Groaning in response, I could feel the anger begin to stir within me. This woman was his mother, the person who was supposed to keep him safe. This woman was the person who was supposed to protect him from anything that would harm him. How could she be so cruel? Staring down at him for a moment, my feeling of anger was swept away, and instead my heart began to fill with tenderness and compassion for the young child and for what he had been through. As Kelly began to help our foster son out of the bathtub, I walked back to the kitchen to resume dinner and retrieve a screaming Melinda from my daughter. Once again, I was reminded that there are so many children who need a foster home and so few homes willing to embrace these children. Fostering is a call, and God's call for families to take care of His children is clear throughout Scripture. To be sure, He wants families to take up His cross and look after His children in need.

A few months later, I attended my foster parent association's annual Christmas party, a time where the foster parents in my county gather together, along with our children (foster, biological, adoptive, and even some grandchildren sprinkled in there). It is a wonderful evening, with great food, fellowship, support, and even an appearance by Santa Claus with gifts for all the children. For all involved, it is a great way to spend the evening as we lift each other up in support and love.

I was able to spend some time chatting with a new set of foster parents who had recently joined our association. This loving husband and wife were parents to 12 children: biological, adoptive, and foster children. I was so impressed by their selflessness and dedication to children as they devoted their lives to helping them. Twelve children! I knew how tired they must have been. Recently, my wife and I had 11 children in our own home. Three of them were biological, three were adoptive, and the remaining five were foster children, a group of siblings that desperately needed a home. Our house was indeed a busy and crazy one, with children ranging in age from 18 months to 16 years, and everything in between. My wife and I knew little rest, and I am sure that this family was in much the same situation.

If truth be known, my wife and I both went to work to rest. Though her job as a massage therapist and doctor of nutrition kept my wife busy, as did my job as a media specialist and school librarian at the local high school in our small rural town of just over 2,000 people, we found the work as foster parents even more demanding. It seemed that when my wife and I both arrived home each evening, we were almost overcome by the mountains of laundry, dinner to cook for a small army, piles of dirty dishes, small children to bathe, homework with which to assist, and everything else that came along with a house full of children. Along with these tasks came trying to help our children from foster care face the daily challenges and traumas with which they struggled from the various horrors that brought them into the foster care system. By the time our heads hit our pillows late each evening, my wife and I were beyond tired, and sleep quickly overcame the both of us.

While traveling across the country working with thousands of foster parents at training conferences and speaking engagements, I continue to meet many such foster parents who are working tirelessly to help children in need. Over and over again, I am inspired by their stories of dedication, unconditional love, and servanthood. The foster parents I met in Texas who only care for babies who are dying from terminal illnesses are one example. They rock these babies in a chair until they die, making sure they are loved until their last breath. Another is the single foster father in South Carolina who only looks after troubled teenage boys. Yet another is the single foster mother in West Virginia who cares for young teenage girls and their babies. These are just a few of the inspirational people I have met through the years, all dedicating their lives to helping children in need and sharing God's love with them.

I have found that society at large does not really understand or appreciate what foster care is. They do not realize what foster children go through each day nor, for that matter, what foster parents go through. Even my own friends and family members do not fully understand what my wife and I experience each day as foster parents, or really why we do it. I even have family members who question why my wife and I continue to take into our hearts and home children who are in need after all these years of sleepless nights and stress-filled days. God's call on my life, though, is a strong one, and one that my wife and I cannot ignore, as I am sure it is for you as well.

Before I was a foster parent, I had some mixed views about the foster care system. To say that I was naïve and ignorant of what foster care is would be quite the understatement. I had two views of foster care. First, foster children were troublemakers, and it was their fault they were in the system. Second, foster parents were pretty weird people. Well, I got one thing correct: the second part. I was really wrong about the first part. Foster parents are pretty weird people, and I have been a foster parent for 12 years as I write this.

We have to be a little weird to do what we do, don't we? After all, foster parents dedicate their lives to serving other people by bringing into their homes and families children who are in need, children who are often troubled, and children who many times have a variety of challenges. To be sure, foster parenting is the hardest thing I have ever done, and continue to do. Perhaps this difficulty is why so few answer the call to be foster parents, as it is a job that requires a great deal of sacrifice from the parent(s) and from the rest of the family.

A successful foster parent is one who provides a caring environment while a birth family works on their caseload, the court-ordered responsibilities that are required for reunification, until the child and birth parent are reunited and living together once again. Foster parents not only provide a caring environment but a safe and stable one as well. During this time, foster parents agree to carry out all functions of the birth family. These day-to-day functions include assuring that the child's medical, nutritional, educational, and parental needs are met. Foster parents may also provide social activities for the child, such as extracurricular events after school, city and county sports, and church-related activities, to name a few. Without question, there can be much joy in being a foster parent. This joy comes from experiences like watching a child in foster care smile for the first time after years of abuse, teaching a child in foster care how to ride a bike, or sharing a foster child's first real birthday with him after so many birthdays have been ignored in the past.

As I wrote in my book *The Foster Parenting Manual*, "Foster parenting is hard work! . . . You will often find yourself exhausted, both mentally and physically . . . There is very little money available to help you, and you will not be reimbursed for all the money you spend on your foster child. The job will require you to work 24 hours a day, seven days a week, with no time off. You will probably feel overworked and underappreciated. You will work with children who are probably coming from difficult and harmful environments. Some of these children will have health issues, some will come with behavioral issues, and some will struggle with learning disabilities. Many times, the children you work with will try your patience and leave you with headaches, frustrations, disappointments, and even heartbreaks. There is a reason why many people are not foster parents, as it is often too difficult. The turnover rate for foster parents in the

United States is between 30 and 50 percent each year (U.S. Department of Health and Human Services 2005)."

There have been those moments when I have questioned whether or not I was making a difference. There have been those times when I have grown frustrated with the system, as I have had to stand by and watch some of the children in my home go back to environments and situations that I knew were not healthy or safe. I have also seen my wife's doubts and her desire to no longer foster as her heart has been broken numerous times as she has grown to love many children, only to see them return to homes where they were once again placed in jeopardy. It is the same for so many foster parents who have shared their stories with me. I have heard from foster parents who lose sleep each night for weeks and months on end, trying to calm and soothe a baby born addicted to crack, heroin, or meth. I have heard from foster parents who have been yelled at on a daily basis from foster teens who are so emotionally upset by their own experiences that they take it out on their foster parents. I have heard from those who have been told one day they could adopt their foster babies, only to be told another day that the baby would return instead to a biological family member the child had never met. The stories are countless, the stories are heartbreaking, and the stories are never ending. Surely, there is no earthly reason to be a foster parent. So, why do we do it? For many, like my wife Kelly and I, we are answering a call.